The Dutch Oven Resource

A Comprehensive Guide to
Dutch Oven Cooking - with Recipes

From the Outdoor Cooking Experts at:

Published By Camp Chef, Logan, UT
Copyright © 2000 By Camp Chef and Gerry & Chauna Duffin

All rights reserved. This book, or parts thereof, may not be reproduced in any form without permission.

First Edition Published 2000 ISBN 0-9709757-0-8
Second Edition Published 2003 ISBN 0-9709757-1-6

Printed in the United States of America

CONTENTS

Introduction 6

Acknowledgements 6

About the Authors 7

PART I - THE BASICS

History 10

What Is A Dutch Oven? 11

Choosing an Oven 12

Seasoning and Maintenance 18

Cleaning a Dutch Oven 22

What If? (Commonly Asked Questions) 24

Tools of the Trade 26

Variables 30

Heat Sources 32

Fire Safety 38

First Aid 38

A Word About Stacking Ovens 39

Camp Chef Products 40

PART II - THE RECIPES

A. Beginning 42

    Breads 46

    Breakfasts 50

    Main Dishes 51

    Desserts 57

B. Intermediate 60

    Breads 64

    Breakfasts 67

    Main Dishes 68

    Desserts 70

C. Advanced 74

    Breads 79

    Main Dishes 82

    Desserts 85

    Garnishing 88

    Cooking for Crowds 90

PART III - ADDITIONAL INFORMATION

IDOS (International Dutch Oven Society) 94

Cooking Courtesy 95

Dutch Oven Cooking at Home 95

Cooking Outdoors 95

Organizing a Club 97

Hosting a Cook-off 97

Judging a Cooking Contest 100

As a Contestant 107

Fixing Problems 108

Safe Food Handling 109

Demonstrations 112

Emergency Preparedness 112

Thermometers 113

Conversions 114

Equivalents 115

Substitutions 115

Afterword 120

Glossary 121

Recipe Index 122

Index 124

INTRODUCTION

Welcome to Dutch oven cooking!

There are many Dutch oven cookbooks on the market. Why another one?

This book is not just a cookbook; it is a resource guide. It will be referred to often by anyone who cooks in a Dutch oven and will answer questions as they arise.

Section I teaches what a Dutch oven is. It covers basic topics such as seasoning and maintenance, helpful tools, heat source usage and much more.

Section II contains recipes for three levels: Beginning, Intermediate and Advanced. Each level has recipes for breads, main dishes and desserts. The Advanced section also has tips for garnishing and cooking for crowds.

Section III has information that up to this point has never been included in a Dutch oven cookbook. This section describes ways to share those cooking skills - organizing a club, hosting a Cook-off and basic food judging guidelines.

We hope this book will help to remove the cloud of mystery that often accompanies Dutch oven cooking. We also hope it will develop confidence and creativity in Dutch oven cooks everywhere.

With all that can be learned here the most important is to have fun!

ACKNOWLEDGMENTS

We have competed, judged, observed, taught and enjoyed the art of Dutch oven cooking. Our lives are richer because of the great people who have shared this hobby with us.

Special thanks to the 'guys' at Camp Chef for the vision and support that made this book possible. Thanks to friends and neighbors for tasting and critiquing our creations.

We especially extend our gratitude to our loving and supportive family for their patience and suggestions.

This book is not just a cookbook; it is a resource guide. It will be referred to often by anyone who cooks in a Dutch oven and will answer questions as they arise.

ABOUT THE AUTHORS

Gerry and Chauna Duffin are from South Jordan, Utah. They enjoy cooking in Dutch ovens and have competed in numerous cook-offs. As successful competitors they have acquired many ribbons and trophies.

They helped compile and are the publishers of the Friends of Old Deseret Dutch Oven Cookbook. They chaired the Old Deseret Dutch Oven Cook-off for several years, which was one of the premier cook-offs in the state of Utah.

They are the owners and operators of Duffin's Dutch Ovens and have organized and taught adult education classes in Dutch oven cooking.

For the Duffin's, Dutch oven cooking has been a family affair, involving more than three generations.

THE BASICS

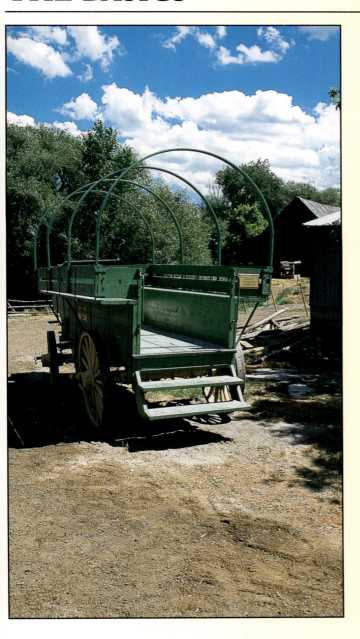

History
What is a Dutch Oven?
Choosing an Oven
Seasoning & Maintenance
Cleaning a Dutch Oven
What If?
  (Commonly Asked Questions)
Tools of the Trade
Variables
Heat Sources
Fire Safety
First Aid
A Word About Stacking Ovens
Camp Chef Products

Best Ever Cinnamon Rolls, page 81.

HISTORY

The Dutch oven, as we know it today, was developed in the early eighteenth century in England and Holland. It is characterized by three legs designed to straddle live coals, a flat-bottomed bowl with flared sides, a rimmed lid to cradle coals on top, and a bail for lifting. This basic design has remained unchanged for centuries, due, no doubt, to the delectable, tender food it produces. There is no need to alter the perfect pot.

The name, however, has had many variations. The functional titles "bake oven," "bake kettle," and "camp oven" all describe how or when the pot is used: baking and camping. The origin of the more common term "Dutch oven" is more elusive. Some writers have argued that the name originated with German and/or Dutch peddlers who sold the cast iron pots from their wagons. Others have credited the Pilgrims with introducing both the pot and the name to this country as a tribute to their former hosts in Holland. A more likely scenario attributes the origin of the name to cast iron cookware made in Holland and imported in to England in the early eighteenth century, or to a Dutch casting technique patented in England in 1708.

Actually, these cast iron kettles might have been more appropriately titled "American ovens," for it was in the great wilderness of the new nation where the pots found their widest use. Dutch ovens were the companions of explorers, trappers, settlers, peddlers, pioneers, miners, soldiers, cowboys, and hunters. Rather than being left behind with the closing of the frontier, the Dutch oven was reincarnated as recreational camping equipment in the twentieth century. In recent years, a surge in popularity has inspired the production of ovens in new or long-abandoned sizes.

(Excerpts from "The Pioneer Art of Dutch Oven Cooking" by Jennifer L. Lund. Friends of Old Deseret Dutch Oven Cookbook, p. 2.)

There is some speculation that Paul Revere, a silversmith by trade, designed the three legs and the raised lip on the lid of our current Camp ovens. We can find no documentation to prove or disprove this tradition.

The aluminum oven is lightweight, transfers heat quickly, requires no seasoning, is dishwasher safe and can withstand rapid changes in temperature.

Cast iron Dutch ovens conduct and retain heat evenly and can withstand higher temperatures than aluminum.

As the kitchen is the heart of the home, the chuckwagon or campfire is the gathering place for outdoor activities. It is a place of comfort and warmth where events of the day or tall tales can be shared. Dutch oven gatherings inspire these same feelings and long-lasting memories.

Aluminum Dutch Oven (Indoor)

WHAT IS A DUTCH OVEN?

Manufacturers use the term "Dutch Oven" for a cast iron or aluminum pot with a smooth bottom and dome shaped lid. A "Camp Oven" is a cast iron or aluminum pot with three legs and a flanged lid. Typically the Dutch oven is used in a conventional oven or on a stovetop. The camp oven is designed for cooking with alternative heat sources such as wood or charcoal briquets.

In the Western United States, the term "Dutch Oven" has evolved to mean any outdoor cooking pot made of cast iron or aluminum. For the purposes of this book, we will be using the term "Dutch Oven" generically to mean both the true Dutch Oven and the Camp Oven. All instructions and recipes can be used for either oven.

DUTCH OVEN MATERIALS

Dutch ovens are commonly made from aluminum or cast iron.

Aluminum Dutch Ovens

The aluminum oven is lightweight, transfers heat quickly, requires no seasoning, is dishwasher safe and can withstand rapid changes in temperature.

Aluminum ovens can warp with too much heat, do not hold the heat as well as cast iron ovens and can react with some acidic foods causing undesirable flavors. When cooking with aluminum, check contents frequently because of rapid heat transfer. It may be necessary to rotate the oven and lid more often.

There has been some controversy over aluminum cookware and Alzheimer's disease. Currently, there is no proof that aluminum cookware is linked to Alzheimer's.

Cast Iron Dutch Ovens

Cast iron Dutch ovens conduct and retain heat evenly and can withstand higher temperatures than aluminum. Well-seasoned cast iron is similar to Teflon®; it prevents food from sticking. The weight of the lid helps to retain moisture. Cast iron is heavy and may break when dropped. Drastic temperature changes will damage cast iron.

CHOOSING AN OVEN

Choosing a Dutch oven is no simple task. In stores that carry a complete line of cast iron, the choice may seem overwhelming. There are round ovens and oval ovens, some with legs and some without, this one has a domed lid and that one has a lip or flanged lid. There are a myriad of sizes, shapes and designs. We hope this section will be helpful for making an informed decision.

THE STORY OF THE UDO®

In 1991 the Ultimate Dutch Oven® was created in response to a health need. The wife of the inventor had a health problem that required a special diet low in fats and oils. They loved Dutch oven cooking but typically used a lot of fat, so they were looking for alternative cooking methods. They found that by adding racks and a center cone to their oven, foods could be cooked with hot air eliminating the need for fats and oils.

When placed over a propane burner, the oven produces delicious food. In 1999, after thoroughly testing the original design, arrangements were made for Camp Chef to produce and market the UDO® with some modifications. It is a natural addition to the Camp Chef line.

The UDO® is manufactured in cast iron and aluminum. The standard UDO® lid is taller than a regular Dutch oven lid, allowing for more cooking options.

How a UDO® Works

- Lid doubles as deep skillet
- Upper rack for versatile baking
- Center cone for oven-like cooking
- Lower rack for roasts and veggies

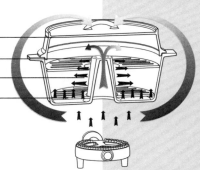

If more headroom is required than a regular lid will provide, turn a similar size oven upside down and use it as a lid. This method is not efficient because the two pots do not form a tight seal, but it will work. We have used this method to cook full prime ribs. It can also be used to cook a whole turkey.

All UDO® lids have legs so they can be used as a skillet. Lids can be used to brown meats, stir fry vegetables, sauté onions, fry eggs and bacon, etc.

There is an optional enhancement kit, which fits the UDO® 14's. It is made of aluminum and has a griddle and a high-rise lid. This actually creates two pots with enough headroom to cook most large poultry or roasts.

Dutch Oven Charts

Most Dutch ovens are measured in quarts. This liquid volume is measured to the rim of the pot. Since there should be approximately 1½-inches of headspace, the functional capacity is less. Headspace is necessary to allow yeast products to raise and brown without touching the lid. Other foods need room for expansion and stirring during cooking.

The following charts list sizes and capacities of various Dutch ovens. Keep in mind that manufacturers' ovens may vary slightly in size, capacity and weight. These serving amounts are approximate since the type of food being cooked can greatly vary the number of servings.

Camp Chef Ovens
Ultimate Dutch Ovens®

Size	Capacity	Depth	Weight	Serves
UDO® 14" Base, Cast Iron	6 qt.	5"	21 1/2 lbs w/racks	16-20
UDO® 14" Lid, Cast Iron	3 1/2 qt.	2 1/2"	14 lbs	
ADO® 14" Base, Aluminum	6 qt.	5"	8 lbs	16-20
ADO® 14" Lid, Aluminum	3 1/2 qt.	2 1/2"	5 lbs	

Advantage Dutch Ovens

Size	Capacity	Depth	Weight	Serves
5" reg	1/2 qt.	2 3/8"	2 1/4 lbs	1-2
5" reg Lid	1/8 qt.	5/8"	1 3/8 lbs	
10" reg	5 qt.	3 7/8"	10 lbs	12-14
10" reg Lid	1 1/8 qt.	7/8"	7 1/2 lbs	
12" reg	7 qt.	4 3/8"	12 1/8 lbs	14-16
12" reg Lid	2 1/3 qt.	1 3/8"	9 1/2 lbs	
14" reg	9 1/8 qt	4 7/8"	14 1/4 lbs	16-20
14" reg Lid	2 3/4 qt.	1 3/8"	10 1/2 lbs	

Classic Dutch Ovens

Size	Capacity	Depth	Weight	Serves
10" reg	4 qt.	3 1/2"	14 lbs	10-12
12" reg	6 qt.	3 3/4"	19 lbs	16-20

Cast Pots

Size	Capacity	Depth	Weight	Serves
10" reg	5 qt.	4 1/4"	12 1/4 lbs	10-12
12" reg	7 qt.	5"	19 lbs	16-20

Enhancement Kit

Size	Capacity	Depth	Weight	Serves
Lid	6 qt.	4"	3 lbs	20
Griddle			1 1/2 lbs	n/a

The Basics

Lodge Camp Ovens
(Legs, Flanged Lid)

Size	Capacity	Depth	Weight	Serves
5" reg	1 pt.	2 1/2"	4 lbs	1 small
8" reg	2 qt.	3"	10 lbs	4-6
10" reg	4 qt.	3 1/2"	14 lbs	10-12
12" reg	6 qt.	3 3/4"	19 lbs	16-20
12" deep	8 qt.	5"	22 lbs	24-28
14" reg	8 qt.	3 3/4"	26 lbs	24-28
14" deep	10 qt.	5"	28 lbs	32-36
16" reg	12 qt.	4 1/2"	38 lbs	36-40

Lodge Standard Dutch Ovens
(No Legs, Dome Lid)

Capacity	Size	Depth	Weight	Serves
2 qt.	8" reg	2 7/8"	8 lbs	12-14
5 qt.	10 1/4" reg	4"	14 lbs	20-22
7 qt.	12" reg	4 3/4"	19 lbs	32-34
9 qt.	13 1/4" reg	4 3/4"	21 lbs	32-34

MACA Supply Custom Ovens

Size	Capacity	Depth	Weight	Serves
9"	5 qt.	6"	16 lbs	13-15
11"	9 qt.	6 1/2"	23 lbs	26-28
13"	12 qt.	6 1/2"	40 lbs	36-38
15"	18 qt.	7 1/2"	48 lbs	57-60
17"	29 qt.	9"	71 lbs	96-100
22"	45 qt.	9 1/2"	158 lbs	160-65
12" x 16"	20 qt.	9"	58 lbs	68-70
8" x 12"	8 qt.	7"	32 lbs	24-28
10" x 14"	14 qt.	8"	45 lbs	44-48

DECIDING WHICH OVEN TO BUY

Before deciding which oven to purchase, ask yourself the following questions:

Will the oven be used indoors?

If cooking will generally be done indoors in a conventional oven or on the stove, choose a Dutch oven without legs and a domed lid. Some domed lids are self-basting. If this feature is desired, check the underside of the lid for several small protrusions. These small spikes collect the moisture and distribute it back onto the food.

The indoor oven is a versatile pot, which can be modified for outdoor use by making a foil ring to hold charcoal on top. The foil ring can be formed by folding a strip of aluminum foil several times until it measures 1-inch wide and is long enough to circle the lid. Overlap the ends and secure with a paper clip. Suspend the pot above the coals with a lid-stand or small cans with both ends removed. Use extra caution with these adaptations to avoid getting ashes in the food.

If cooking will generally be done outdoors, the camp oven is best. Look for an oven with three legs and a flanged lid. It can be adapted for indoor use by adjusting conventional oven racks to allow air circulation around the Dutch oven. Make sure the Dutch oven is firmly seated. If the Dutch oven legs will not fit through the wires of the rack, a cookie sheet placed on the rack will provide proper support.

How many will I typically feed?

Refer to the charts on pages 12 & 13 for Dutch oven sizes and approximate number of servings. The 12-inch regular Dutch oven is the most popular size. Dutch oven recipes are typically written for this size oven and other recipes are easily adapted because it has the same capacity as a 9-inch by 13-inch casserole pan.

As skills increase, so will the need for more Dutch ovens. Often it is necessary to use three Dutch ovens at the same time - one for main dish, one for breads, and one for desserts.

Check for pits (small holes) inside where food can collect. If the casting is uneven, avoid that oven - it will not transfer heat uniformly. If the oven is in a box, open it and inspect before purchasing. If it is not possible to open the box, make sure it can be returned if not satisfactory.

A tight fitting lid works similar to a pressure cooker, keeping moisture and flavors in.

What if I do a lot of baking?
For baking, regular ovens are best. In most cases, baked goods will brown better if they are closer to the heat source. Deep ovens can be used for baking by adding a few more briquets to the lid to allow for extra headspace.

What heat source will I use?
Charcoal, propane, conventional oven and firewood are the most common heat sources. All Dutch ovens can be used with any type of heat. For more information, see the section on Heat Sources.

How much should I spend?
Education is the key to proper Dutch oven selection. Learn about manufacturing methods. Check out different brands of cast iron on the Internet. Ask people who frequently use Dutch ovens which brand they recommend. The purchase of a Dutch oven is an investment that, with proper care, will last a lifetime. Take the time to consider all the factors, not just the price.

Where can I purchase a Dutch oven?
Dutch ovens are usually seasonal items for grocery stores and can normally be found year 'round in sporting goods stores and war surplus stores. If not available locally, contact a store manager about the possibility of a special order or surf the web.

WHAT TO LOOK FOR IN A DUTCH OVEN
Once an oven size has been selected, check for the following:

Does the lid fit correctly?
With the lid on the pot, place hands on opposite sides of the lid and push down to make sure it doesn't rock. Lids or pots can be warped or have other defects. Check for a snug fit that will not allow moisture to escape during cooking.

Is the casting uniform?
Not all Dutch ovens are created equal! Check the sidewalls by placing fingers on the inside of the oven while holding the thumb on the outside and running the hand around the pot. Major problems with casting will be felt.

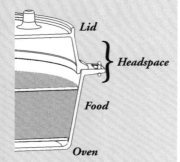

SEASONING CAST IRON

The purpose of seasoning is to create a slick non-stick surface by filling the open pores of the cast iron. This will allow for easy clean up, inhibit rust, and provide a surface that will not react with the food being cooked. This finish or shiny black surface is called the patina.

With proper use and care, Dutch ovens become better with use.

If a sticky Dutch oven results, too much seasoning product has been applied or the oven was not heated long enough or hot enough. Put the cast iron back in the heat source and re-heat.

WARNING: ALWAYS USE EXTREME CAUTION WHEN SEASONING OVENS. KEEP CHILDREN AND PETS AWAY. HAVE HOT PADS OR HEAVY LEATHER GLOVES AVAILABLE TO HANDLE HOT OVENS.

IN CASE OF BURNS, KEEP FIRST AID SUPPLIES NEARBY.

SEASONING OVENS PRODUCES SMOKE AND CAN SET OFF SMOKE ALARMS. PROVIDE PLENTY OF VENTILATION BY OPENING DOORS AND WINDOWS.

ALL CAST IRON NEEDS TO BE SEASONED OR CURED.

If the Dutch oven gets too hot, all seasoning products will burn off. If this happens, allow the oven to cool enough to handle, re-apply seasoning product and re-heat. Carefully watch time and temperature to avoid repeating the error.

Un-seasoned cast iron

Seasoned cast iron

These products should be stored at approximately 70°

SHAKE WELL
BEFORE USING

These instructions are for a 12" regular Dutch oven. Adjust as necessary for larger or smaller ovens.

If using indoors, place a drip tray under cast iron and allow plenty of ventilation. Burning wax will smoke.

USING CAMP CHEF CAST IRON CLEANER AND CONDITIONER

Camp Chef Cleaner®
This product takes the place of soap without the side effects, perfumes or soapsuds. It leaves no residue and works as a surfactant to loosen food particles and to clean all cast iron.

Camp Chef Conditioner®
This new product is superior in seasoning cast iron cookware. It fills the pores better and builds patina faster than using shortening or oils. It does not go rancid when left over long periods, as other oils do. It is an all-natural plant-based product. When used according to the following directions, this product will produce excellent results.

For a New Oven
Scour your Dutch oven with HOT water and an abrasive steel wool and soap pad to remove the factory applied wax coating. If the wax coating is thick and does not easily wash off, burn it off by using a propane stove, gas barbecue or conventional oven. Heat to approximately 350° until cast iron no longer smokes. Let cool and continue to next step.

Rinse thoroughly with HOT tap water.

Put approximately 1 quart of HOT water in your Dutch oven and add 1 tablespoon of Cleaner. Mix thoroughly. Wash all surfaces of oven and lid.

Rinse again with HOT water.

Blot dry using paper towels or cloth - DO NOT RUB. (Rubbing will leave lint on cast iron surfaces.)

While oven is still warm, apply approximately 1 tablespoon conditioner to all surfaces by hand. (Paper towels will leave lint.) If desired, a lint-free cloth may be used but the cloth will absorb more conditioner.

For Previously Seasoned Ovens
If current seasoning is sound, apply approximately 1/2 teaspoon conditioner to the inside surface of the oven and lid. Blot any excess with a paper towel. Place a clean paper towel in the oven to absorb any moisture. Place the lid ajar and store.

If current seasoning is not satisfactory, the symptoms will be black flakes in food, metallic taste, and/or food sticking to the surfaces. Remove the old patina by placing the Dutch oven and lid upside down in a self-cleaning oven. Run through a cleaning cycle, or place in a barbecue on high.

When cool enough to remove, follow instructions for seasoning a new Dutch oven.

OTHER PRODUCTS AND METHODS

Some people use products such as lard or oil and are satisfied with the results. We prefer the Camp Chef Seasoning and Conditioner®. If they are not available, an alternative is white Crisco® shortening, as described below. All other products, for various reasons, are more difficult to apply or do not produce the desired finish.

Shortening Method

Use white Crisco® shortening and apply a thin coat to all surfaces (inside and out). Place in a conventional oven, upside down with lid leaning against pot. Set temperature to 400° for approximately 30 minutes or until cast iron no longer smokes. It may be necessary to apply more than one coat to achieve the desired patina. To avoid injury, allow oven to cool between coats.

Barbecue Method

We prefer this method because one coat produces the beautiful patina that requires several coats in an oven. The inevitable smoking during seasoning is outside, leaving the house smoke-free.

Sometimes it is necessary to remove the upper cooking rack and lava rocks from the barbecue (do not remove the bottom rack) so the Dutch oven will fit when the lid is closed. Place the prepared Dutch oven upside down on the rack in the center of the barbecue. Place the lid upside down, leaning against one of the legs of the Dutch oven.

Set the barbecue to medium heat. Close the lid. After approximately 10 minutes, check to see if the Dutch oven is smoking. If not, increase the temperature. After 20-30 minutes, the smoking should stop. Turn the barbecue off and let the oven cool. This will result in a hard, black, easy-to-clean coating.

Propane Stove Method

Because of the direct flame, it is possible to over-heat an oven and burn the seasoning products off. It is also possible that all surfaces will not season evenly. This is normal.

Place the prepared Dutch oven upside down over a propane stove (we suggest 30,000 BTU) for approximately 15-20 minutes on medium heat. After 5-10 minutes, the Dutch oven should start to smoke and change color. When the oven stops smoking, turn the burner off. Let the oven cool. Season the lid separately using the same method. This method works well for larger ovens.

Some people use products such as lard or oil and are satisfied with the results. We prefer the Camp Chef Conditioner® and Cleaner.

The Basics

For availability of Camp Chef Cleaner and Conditioner®, contact the Camp Chef dealer in your area or call Camp Chef direct at: 1-800-783-8347

For the first few times after seasoning your oven, it is best not to cook foods high in acid. This will weaken the seasoning.

Season just before bedtime so oven can cool overnight.

Camp Fire Method

We do not recommend using a campfire to season a Dutch oven because it has too many variables. The fire and heat are not consistent and soot from the fire could turn the Dutch oven black while not actually seasoning the oven.

Oven Method

It is not necessary to preheat the conventional oven.

Place the Dutch oven upside down on a rack in the center of a conventional oven. Place the lid upside down, leaning on one of the legs of the Dutch oven. (This will allow any excess seasoning product to drip off.) A cookie sheet can be placed on the bottom rack to catch any excess conditioning product.

Set the oven to 425° for Camp Chef conditioner and 400° for shortening, 425° is too hot for shortening, it will burn off. Open windows to allow adequate ventilation. This will smoke. After 20-25 minutes, check to make sure the cast iron is smoking. Continue heating until smoking stops.

Leave the Dutch oven in the conventional oven until cool.

This method will produce an amber to black color and is ready for cooking.

Seasoning an Aluminum Oven

Aluminum Dutch ovens do not need to be seasoned. They should be washed thoroughly with soap and hot water before use.

DO'S

Do use a hard plastic scraper to scrape out any excess food after cooking (sharp metal utensils will damage the patina).

Do use a whiskbroom to remove ashes from the outside of the oven.

Do wash the outside surface of your oven. A vegetable brush works well for the exterior.

Do use hot tap water to clean the inside of your oven. If the oven still isn't clean after rinsing with water or is greasy, add 2-quarts of hot tap water; use a plastic cleaning pad or kitchen brush and scrub. If greasy, use a couple of drops of dish soap that doesn't contain perfumes. Wash with a dishrag. Rinse several times with hot tap water and dry with a paper towel or lint free cloth.

Do use Camp Chef Cleaner®. (See section on Camp Chef Cleaner and Conditioner®.) When using the cleaner, follow these simple directions: Rinse ash from the outside surfaces of your oven. Put approximately 2-quarts of hot tap water into the oven and add 2 tablespoons of cleaner. Mix well. Wash thoroughly. Drain. Rinse with hot water and dry.

CLEANING A DUTCH OVEN

There are just about as many opinions on how to clean a Dutch oven as there are Dutch oven cooks.

Dirty or rancid Dutch ovens are not healthy.

All Dutch ovens should be cleaned as soon as possible after use.

Waiting makes them difficult to clean and promotes rust.

A clean Dutch oven is essential for producing good food!

LONG TERM DUTCH OVEN STORAGE

If storing for several months, make sure the oven is clean and dry. Excess oil will go rancid or sticky. This is where the Camp Chef conditioner really 'shines'. It does not go rancid like other oils. If possible, store the lid and pot separate to allow air circulation. If not possible, place newspaper or paper towels in the oven. Place the lid ajar.

ROUTINE CLEANING

Don'ts

Don't put cast iron in the dishwasher. Those who do not want to wash Dutch ovens by hand should buy aluminum ovens.

Don't use salt to clean cast iron. Salt is very abrasive and corrosive. If there is any moisture is in the oven, salt will have a tendency to pit and rust the oven.

Don't use a lot of soap to clean an oven, especially soaps with perfumes; the next dish prepared will taste like the soap used for cleaning. However, contrary to some die-hard Dutch oven cooks, it will not hurt cast iron to use one or two drops of dish soap in a Dutch oven full of hot water after cooking a greasy meal. In a properly seasoned oven it will cut the grease and if rinsed well, will leave no soapy residue or lingering flavors. Honest!

Don't use metal scrapers, steel scouring pads or other abrasive products to remove stubborn food particles. These items could damage the seasoning.

Don't use oily rags to wipe the exterior of an oven until it has been thoroughly cleaned.

Don't allow an oven to air dry. Dry it immediately with paper towels or a lint free cloth to avoid rust. Better yet, heat the oven again to evaporate all moisture.

Don't soak an oven for an extended period in soapy dishwater. It will penetrate the pores of the oven and is difficult to remove.

Don't shock cast iron with extreme temperatures. In other words, don't pour cold liquid in a hot Dutch oven or place a cold Dutch oven over extreme heat. This can crack or break the oven. Cast iron needs to change temperature gradually.

Don't cook on surfaces that can be damaged by the heat. Asphalt will melt, concrete and wood decks can be scarred and lawns can be burned. Make sure there is a barrier (see equipment listing) between hot charcoal and other surfaces.

Don't re-oil your oven after every use. If the seasoning becomes dull, apply on a very light coat of oil or Camp Chef Conditioner® to restore a satin finish. (Too much oil will leave your oven sticky and will go rancid.)

WHAT IF?

What if my oven is rusty?

Rust can be removed by one of the following methods:

<u>Mildly rusty.</u> Scrub with a product like SOS® (soap on steel wool pads).

<u>Moderately rusty.</u> Boil interior surfaces with tomato juice or soak in cola.

<u>Severely rusty.</u> Use of a drill and a wire wheel will usually be sufficient to remove the rust or take the oven to someone who can sand blast all surfaces.

What if my seasoning is flaking off?

If there are black specks in the food (and it's not pepper), the seasoning is deteriorating and should be removed. The best and easiest way to remove seasoning is to use a self-cleaning oven. The self-cleaning cycle will totally strip the Dutch oven.

If a self-cleaning oven is not available, this can also be done on a propane burner. Turn the Dutch oven upside down on the propane burner over medium heat until all the seasoning burns off. If the seasoning is heavy, more heat and time may be required to strip the Dutch oven. Lids must be stripped separately.

Warning: Don't use high settings. This can warp or crack the oven or lid.

The least desirable method for stripping a Dutch oven is turning it upside-down in a campfire. There is no control over the temperature. Campfires can ruin your cast iron, causing warping, distortion, cracking and breaks.

What if my food has a metallic taste?

Dutch ovens that are improperly seasoned or seasoning that is beginning to break down will cause a metallic taste in any food cooked. The best remedy is to strip the Dutch oven and re-season it.

ALWAYS REMEMBER TO RE-SEASON A DUTCH OVEN IMMEDIATELY AFTER REMOVING RUST!

The Basics

The inside surfaces of cast iron do not need to be perfectly smooth. It is only necessary to remove any burrs or extremely rough spots. Seasoning and use will eventually produce a worn and even surface.

If a burr can be seen on the oven or lid, this can be removed with a metal file. When finished, be sure to thoroughly clean the oven.

What if my Dutch oven is rancid or sticky?

Too much oil is being left in the oven. Try the following:

Wash the oven thoroughly with hot water; boil if necessary.

Put the Dutch oven over a heat source like a propane burner or barbecue and heat until it no longer smokes.

If the oven is still sticky or rancid, completely strip the Dutch oven as described in the cleaning section and start over.

What if I have burned food in my Dutch oven?

This is a very difficult problem to solve, depending on the severity. We suggest trying one of the following methods: (At this point, there is nothing to lose.)

Try boiling water to soften the burned food, add one or two teaspoons baking soda.

A self-clean cycle in a conventional oven should turn it to ash.

Try lots of elbow grease and an SOS® or scouring pad.

What if the inside of my oven is too rough?

One solution is to take it to a machine shop and have it machined. This could be expensive but would give a smooth surface.

The most economical solution is to sand by hand with emery cloth using at least 100 grit. This may take several sheets. It is labor-intensive but will eventually smooth the surface.

What if my lid doesn't fit right?

Those who purchase or inherit an oven with minor lid problems can use valve-lapping compound. This product is available at hardware or automotive stores. Place a bead of valve-lapping compound on the lip of the pot. Set the lid on the oven. Spin the lid by hand until the desired fit is achieved. This may take several minutes and is only for mildly warped or rough ovens.

What if my Dutch oven is cracked? Can it be repaired?

A cracked lid or pot may allow moisture to escape or collect food particles. It is a weak spot that may be hazardous when the pot is hot and full of food.

Cast iron is very difficult to weld. It is hard to find someone who knows the proper technique. We suggest you "chalk it up to experience" and buy a new Dutch oven.

TOOLS OF THE TRADE

As in any hobby or skill the right tools will make the job easier. Dutch oven cooking is no exception. It is not necessary to purchase all of these tools at once.

Necessities
Lid Lifter
There are several types available. Find one that is comfortable to hold and allows good control of the cast iron, especially the lid. We like the 'Mair Lifter' manufactured by A & B Manufacturing in Midway, Utah. This lifter comes in a short and long model. The long model is for cooking at ground level or on an open fire. The short model is for cooking on raised surfaces. It has a grip system that allows positive control as long as the handle is squeezed. This is especially important when the lid is covered with hot charcoal or when dumping spent ashes. Many Dutch oven lids have been damaged by the use of makeshift lid lifters, i.e. claw hammers, channel locks, etc. For best results, use the right tool for the job.

Tongs
For handling hot charcoal, 16-inch heavy-duty stainless steel tongs with a clamshell end are best. Use separate tongs for food handling.

Heavy Welding Gloves
A pair of welding gloves is a must to safely handle anything hot.

Lid-stand
Never place Dutch oven lids on the ground! A lid-stand keeps lids and pots from being contaminated with dirt, leaves or grass. It is also great for keeping hot pots off tabletops. A good lid stand is versatile and can be used with an inverted lid as a cooking surface for pancakes, crepes, etc.

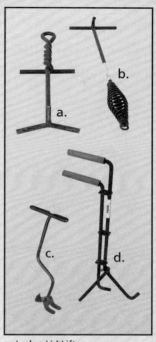

a. Lodge Lid Lifter,
b. Twin K Lid Lifter,
c. Camp Chef Lid Lifter,
d. Mair Lid Lifter

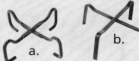

a. Lodge Lid Stand,
b. Twin K Lid Lid Stand

To keep this cookbook in good condition, select the desired recipe, fold the book in half and slip it inside a quart or gallon size Ziplock® bag. The bag becomes a spill proof cover and storage container.

There are several variations on the market. Some have curved feet to protect ovens and lids from scratching. Some fold up for storage. They all do basically the same thing so find one that best fits your needs.

Heat-resistant Surface for Cooking
Charcoal and other fuels used in Dutch oven cooking get extremely hot. Asphalt, concrete, wood decks and lawns can be damaged. Use a protective surface such as old cookie sheets, drum lids, several layers of heavy-duty foil or stepping stones.

Cleaning Kit
Assemble the following items into a container for quick and easy clean up:

A plastic scraper

Plastic mesh scouring pad

Steel wool soap pad for rusty ovens, or new ovens

Vegetable brush – good for inside and outside surfaces

Camp Chef Cleaner and Conditioner®

Paper towels

Dutch Oven Cookbook
An unfamiliar destination is difficult to find without the use of a quality road map or atlas. A good Dutch oven cookbook can be used in the same way. It is not necessary to buy ONLY Dutch oven cookbooks. Once the information in this book is learned, almost any recipe can be used in Dutch oven cooking.

There are many books on the market. Select one that has complete instructions and quality recipes.

Optional Items
Cooking Table
A good cooking table is tall enough to keep cooking at a convenient height. It should be strong enough to support the weight of several Dutch ovens and be able to withstand heat without warping. Legs should be adjustable to accommodate uneven surfaces.

Small Level
To avoid lop-sided dishes, keep a small level with your equipment to level the cooking surface.

All-Purpose Stove
The All-Purpose Stove (APS) is a portable multi-purpose cooking apparatus, which uses charcoal as a heat source. The versatility of this item continues to grow. It's foldout design provides for easy transport, quick set-up and safe, efficient cooking. By itself, the APS can barbecue or you can add a skillet or wok. Dutch oven cooking uses less charcoal because of its efficient design. Add an Ultimate Dutch Oven® with the enhancement kit and the possibilities are endless.

The safe design allows for cooking on combustible surfaces. The exterior surface does not get hot enough to cause damage—you can cook right on your table top.

Tool Hanger
A tool hanger is a device which will keep lid lifters, whisk brooms and other miscellaneous tools handy while cooking.

Charcoal Basket
A charcoal basket is a quick and convenient way to start charcoal over propane.

Chimney Starter
A metal cylinder used to start charcoal with newspaper or lighter fluid. The charcoal is placed in the top on a grate. It can then be sprinkled with lighter fluid and lit. Alternatively, newspaper is inserted underneath and lit.

Dutch Oven Covers or Totes
Covers are commonly made of heavy nylon or canvas fabric to protect and store Dutch ovens.

Wire Rack or Trivet
Racks or trivets are used to keep meats out of grease during cooking or steamed items above liquids. Made of heavy wire or cast iron, they can also be used to hold pans or other cooking items above the bottom of the oven. The Camp Chef Ultimate Dutch Oven® incorporates grates similar to this as part of its design.

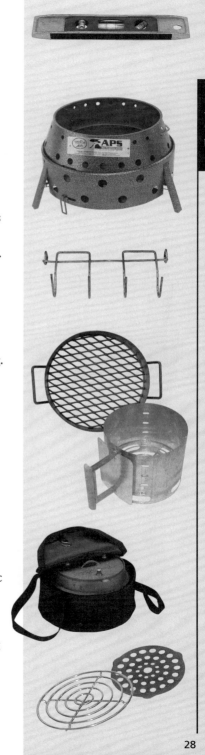

ID Tags
Identification tags make it possible to keep lids and pots together as a set. They are also valuable in assuring the right Dutch oven is returned to its owner when borrowed.

Instant Read Thermometer
A good thermometer is a must for determining when your food is done. See the section on food safety, located on page 107 for more information.

Whisk Broom
These small brooms are excellent for cleaning ashes off ovens and other equipment.

Ash Bucket and Shovel
A heavy metal bucket combined with a small square shovel used for safe handling of charcoal and ashes until they can be disposed of properly.

Grub Box/Camp Kitchen
Those who often cook outdoors will appreciate a grub box or camp kitchen. There are as many different designs as there are cooks. Some people build a wooden cupboard with a place for cooking paraphernalia. Others keep it simple with a 5-gallon bucket lined with fabric pockets. We use large plastic containers with lids; one is filled with food supplies while the other contains preparation materials.

Tool Box for Utensils
For convenience place all cooking and serving tools in one central location. This portable container can be whatever works best. We use a large toolbox with removable trays.

Make sure it can be cleaned, sanitized and organized for easy access. This is the place to keep those ladles, large serving spoons, sharp knives (with shields for protection), measuring cups and spoons, first aid supplies, etc. At our house, these items are separate from our home kitchen supplies.

Box For Transporting Dutch Ovens
This is something handy for those who cook at home and want to transport the finished product. Because ovens have three legs, they are unstable in the trunk of a car. A wooden box can give the security needed to be sure the food arrives safely.

VARIABLES

Altitude

The two most important factors in cooking at high altitudes are time and temperature. It may be necessary to cook foods longer and/or at higher temperatures in order to reach the required internal temperature. Contact your local county extension office for more information on altitude cooking.

Here are a few basic tips:

Baking: (Most recipes are written for sea level 0')

Cookies need little adjustment in ingredients but need about 20° more heat for a shorter cooking time to keep them from drying out.

Biscuits and muffins need slightly less sugar and baking powder and slightly more liquid. (Liquids evaporate faster at high altitudes.)

Cakes with a higher fat content or lots of chocolate may need less shortening (1 to 2 tablespoons less) and an additional egg to keep them from falling. Cakes also need about 20° more heat and a shorter cooking time to keep them from expanding too much. If cooking at 3,000 feet, add 1 - 2 tablespoons additional liquid and decrease sugar about 1 tablespoon. For 5,000 feet add 2 - 4 tablespoons liquid and decrease sugar 1 - 2 tablespoons. For 7,000 feet, add 3 - 4 tablespoons liquid and decrease sugar 2 - 3 tablespoons.

Flours tend to absorb more liquid and be drier at high altitudes.

Wind

Wind can literally blow heat away. In windy conditions, provide a windbreak or protection for Dutch ovens. (See Camp Chef cooking table with windscreen.) It may be necessary to rearrange charcoal. Wind can act as a bellows for charcoal causing hot spots. Rotate ovens more often and check frequently. It may also be necessary to replenish charcoal since wind causes it to burn hotter and faster.

Breads seem to be the most sensitive to windy conditions and require constant attention.

Liquids boil at lower temperatures and evaporate more quickly at high altitudes. Add a little extra liquid and cook for a longer time, but do not increase the cooking temperature.

The Basics

Cold Weather (Snow)
Cold, wet weather makes it difficult to keep charcoal going. Keep plenty of hot coals handy; it will probably be necessary to add more during cooking. Remember hot pots and extreme cold temperatures can cause problems. Never place a hot oven in cold water or snow and never place cold cast iron directly over high heat. Bring temperatures up gradually.

Hot Weather (Sunshine)
A black cast iron pot on a hot sunny day will require less charcoal. Reduce charcoal by one on the bottom and two on top. Check the food often. If it is still cooking too hot, reduce again. Be careful with yeast products. The heat of the oven by itself may be enough to kill the yeast. Keep ovens out of direct sun until dough has doubled and is ready to cook.

Humidity (Rain)
Always provide shelter in the rain. Damp charcoal is hard to light and less efficient. More charcoal may be required to maintain temperatures.

HEAT SOURCES

WARNING! FOR SAFETY, USE EXTREME CAUTION WHEN HANDLING ANY HEAT SOURCE. TO AVOID ACCIDENTS, MAKE SURE COOKING AREAS ARE CLEAR OF OBSTRUCTIONS AND COMBUSTIBLE MATERIALS. CHARCOAL BRIQUETS ARE EXTREMELY HOT AND CAN CAUSE SEVERE BURNS. NEVER ALLOW SMALL CHILDREN OR PETS NEAR HOT DUTCH OVENS OR CHARCOAL.

WHEN CAMPING, ALWAYS CHECK FIRE AND FUEL RESTRICTIONS.

CHARCOAL

Charcoal briquets are the easiest and most reliable heat source for cooking with Dutch ovens. We have tried many brands and have found Kingsford® Regular to be the most reliable, consistent and longest burning.

Kingsford Charcoal History

Being the frugal person that he was, Henry Ford invented the pillow-shaped briquets in an effort to use up wood scraps from the production of his cars. Kingsford charcoal is a combination of wood charcoal, anthracite coal, mineral charcoal, starch, sodium nitrate, limestone, sawdust and borax. These are all combined under strict manufacturing guidelines to produce a quality, long-lasting, hot-burning briquet.

Kingsford charcoal will last approximately 45 minutes to 1 hour depending on weather conditions. If a dish requires longer than 1 hour to cook, replace charcoal as necessary to maintain a constant temperature. When calculating the amount of charcoal needed, a 10-pound bag contains approximately 150 to 180 briquets. Each briquet provides approximately 12-15° of heat.

Here are a few charcoal basics:

Charcoal will burn hotter when it is kept dry.

Ash can act as an insulator, trapping heat inside. Lightly tap ash covered briquets to release heat.

Briquet pattern for Baking with a 12" Dutch oven

Top

Bottom

The entire charcoal does not need to be gray in order to begin cooking. When half of the briquet is started, it is useable. It will continue heating until the entire briquet is lit.

The number of charcoal and their placement is the key to proper Dutch oven cooking. Always start a few extra briquets in case conditions require additional heat

Baking with Charcoal

The "plus 4, minus 4" rule is a good starting point for charcoal distribution when baking. This means the size of the Dutch oven (the number usually appears on the lid) plus four charcoals for top heat and the size of the Dutch oven minus four charcoals for bottom heat.

Example:
12-inch Dutch oven + 4 = 16 for top heat and 12-inch - 4 = 8 for bottom heat.

Bottom charcoal placement for all ovens (except the 16-inch) should be a circular pattern placed just inside the bottom edge of the pot and evenly spaced. For the lid, evenly space most of the charcoal around the rim with a smaller circular pattern around the handle.

Example:
A 12-inch Dutch oven uses 24 briquets. For bottom placement, 8 charcoal are used in a circular pattern. For lid placement, 10 are used for the outside ring and 6 around the handle.

Rotate the oven clockwise a quarter of a turn every 10-15 minutes and the lid counter clockwise. This will produce even heating. For bottom heat, <u>avoid placing charcoal directly in the center.</u> Heat from outside briquets radiates inward, eliminating the need for a center briquet.

The one exception to the above rule is the 16-inch oven. Because it is so large, a checkerboard pattern underneath seems to work best. Be sure to rotate the oven.

It's okay to rearrange your charcoal as necessary. If you find a place not raising evenly or browning as it should, move some heat to it. If there is a hot spot, rotate the oven or rearrange heat.

Roasting with Charcoal
Use the same number of briquets on both the top and bottom of the oven as the size of the oven. Example: On a 12-inch Dutch oven, use 12 briquets on top and 12 on bottom.

Boiling, Steaming, Simmering and Frying with Charcoal
These methods require a different charcoal placement called a checkerboard pattern and use bottom heat only.

Storing Charcoal
Charcoal will store indefinitely if kept in a cool, dark, dry place. Five-gallon buckets with tight-fitting lids make great storage containers.

Starting Charcoal
Starting charcoal can sometimes be a challenge. There is nothing more frustrating than trying to cook with charcoal that will not light or stay lit. Here are some methods we have found helpful:

Starting Charcoal with Commercial Lighter Fluid
This is the slowest and least reliable method. It also has an unpleasant odor. Pile the number of charcoal needed on a non-combustible surface and sprinkle generously with lighter fluid. Light carefully. When using this method, start charcoal 20-30 minutes in advance.

WARNING: For your safety, never add lighter fluid after you have initially lit the briquets. Use only lighter fluid manufactured specifically for charcoal. Never use gasoline or other flammable liquids

Starting Charcoal Using a Chimney Lighter
This method can present a fire hazard because burning newspaper has a tendency to scatter ashes. Place a couple of sheets of crumpled newspaper in the bottom portion of the starter. Place the required number of briquets in the top and light the newspaper. Charcoal will be ready in 15-25 minutes.

Chimneys can also be set over propane stoves for lighting charcoal.

Briquet pattern for Roasting with a 12" Dutch oven

Top

Bottom

It's really a simple process to adjust your heat when cooking. As our friend Dellis Hatch says: "If it's not cooking fast enough, add more heat. If it's cooking too fast, take some off." Good advice!

34

Open Fire Cooking Instructions:

Spread a layer of hot embers across an elongated rectangle. Place prepared Dutch oven over embers. Shovel another layer of embers evenly on the lid. Rotate pot and lid every 10-15 minutes. Replenish embers as necessary. Continue cooking until food is done.

Keyhole Fire diagram

Using a Charcoal Basket

We prefer this method because it is a quick way to provide a constant supply of fresh charcoal. A charcoal basket is a metal cylinder with an expanded metal bottom, which can be placed over a propane burner or other heat source to ignite charcoal. Place desired number of briquets in the basket, set over heat source and wait approximately five minutes.

Disposing of Charcoal

A coal bucket can be used to hold hot briquets and ashes until ready for disposal. Make sure it is placed on concrete or some other non-combustible surface. When disposing of hot charcoal, it is best to gradually dump the charcoal into water rather than water onto charcoal. Stir after each addition using a metal shovel. Water dumped onto charcoal can explode and cause serious injury. After coals and ashes are cooled, they are safe to pour out and are not harmful to the environment. Be sure charcoal is completely cooled. We have heard of fires caused by charcoal that was not properly extinguished.

Warning: Never cook inside with charcoal. A by-product of combustion is deadly carbon monoxide, which is an odorless, invisible killer.

PROPANE STOVE

This fuel source is for bottom heat only. It is good for grilling, boiling, frying, starting charcoal, etc. Camp Chef's Ultimate Dutch Oven® is designed for easy use on a propane stove.

OPEN FIRE COOKING

Many factors will affect cooking temperatures when using coals from a fire. Hardwoods burn hotter and longer than soft. Dry wood burns hotter than damp. Always use coals rather than the direct flame. Some believe that burning out an oven is a good way to clean it, we don't recommend it.

For open fire cooking, we suggest a keyhole fire. A keyhole fire is shaped like the keyhole of an old-fashioned lock. There is a circle at the top (A) and a small elongated rectangle at the bottom (B). The fire is made in the circle (A) and as the wood becomes hot embers, they are placed in the elongated rectangle (B). This must be replenished as needed to supply constant embers for cooking.

BURYING DUTCH OVENS

In days gone by, some shepherds buried their Dutch ovens leaving them to cook all day while tending sheep. They would return in the evening to a nice hot meal. Some people believe this is the only way to cook in a Dutch oven. It is only ONE way.

Dig a hole deep enough to accommodate the Dutch oven AND twelve inches of coals. Six inches of coals will be on the bottom and six inches will be on the top of the oven. A 16 to 18-inch hole will usually suffice.

Build two campfires: one inside the hole, and one just outside and near the hole. The fire inside the hole is very important. The hole must be hot or it will absorb much of the heat from the coals when the oven is buried. If this happens, the meal will be a disaster!

Do not use charcoal briquets in place of firewood. The briquets will stop burning when covered with dirt.

While the fires are burning, prepare the entrée. If cooking a roast, be sure to preheat the oven and sear all sides of the roast before lowering it into the pit. Searing helps meats retain natural juices.

When baking desserts or breads, it is not necessary to preheat the oven. Let bread dough rise in the oven prior to burying.

When the entrée is prepared, cover the lid with heavy-duty tin foil. Allow the foil to drape down around the side of the oven. When it is time to unveil the cooked product, the dirt and ashes will be contained as the foil is peeled away.

Be sure there are at least six inches of hot coals in the pit. Lower the oven into the pit and then shovel the other campfire coals onto and around the oven. Then cover the whole thing with dirt. If you are leaving the area for a few hours, be sure to place a marker right over the buried oven so you'll know exactly where to dig when retrieving it.

Let the oven stay in the ground for at least five hours. It can stay there for up to eight hours and still be piping hot. If longer than eight hours, reheating may be necessary. Plan meal times within eight hours of burying.

An Elk roast surrounded with vegetables is a favorite when cooked this way. After searing the roast, place the veggies around and on top of it.

Mix one dry packet of meat marinade and one dry packet of teriyaki seasoning to a quart of water. Pour the water in the oven so the water level is even with the top of the roast. It may be necessary to add more water to reach this level. Any roast will do well using this approach.

We turned to an expert for this section and thank our friend and Dutch oven cook, Sid Lawrence, for these instructions.

Cooking with a Dutch oven in the kitchen

KITCHEN OVEN

What? Dutch oven cooking in the kitchen? This is one of the best places to use a Dutch oven. In fact it is where the true Dutch oven was designed to be used. The kitchen is always available, the oven can provide a constant heat source and is convenient. Adjust racks so the Dutch oven is centered. For a true Dutch oven (no legs), no adjustments are necessary. For a Camp oven, place the legs between the wires of the rack so the pot sits flat. If adjustment is difficult, place a large cookie sheet under the legs. Set the temperature to 350º.

Since a Dutch oven will usually cook a little faster than other cookware, check meats at least one-half hour before normal cooking time ends. For baked goods that need to brown, leave the Dutch oven lid off. Baked goods may be done 10-15 minutes before the end of normal cooking time.

BUFFALO CHIPS

With our friends, Tony and Jenny Lund, we had the once-in-a-lifetime opportunity of cooking with buffalo chips. The smoke from the buffalo chips drifted into the air conditioning intake of a nearby office building and the occupants thought the building was on fire. (Oops!)

When the pioneers were coming west, children were often sent out to gather buffalo chips for cooking. Contrary to what might be expected, the smell of burning chips is similar to that of burning grass. Buffalo chips produce a lot of smoke and do not burn as long or as hot as charcoal. It takes a large supply to cook a meal.

For those who happen to live in an area where buffalo roam, gather a gunnysack full of chips (make sure they are thoroughly dry and gather plenty) and have fun!

Instructions for Using Buffalo Chips:

Make a keyhole fire as described in the section for a wood fire. That fire will be the source of coals. Rotate chips through until they smolder. Chips must be replaced often to produce consistent heat.

FIRE SAFETY

Always be aware of the danger of fire when working with charcoal or any other heat source. Keep a safe distance from any flammable surfaces. Several years ago, a family came home from church to a burning house because they had left dinner cooking on a wooden deck, unattended.

Protect yourself and others by keeping the heat contained. Throughout this book, we have included warnings and cautions, Please heed them so that every cooking experience will be a safe one.

A fire extinguisher is always a valuable piece of equipment to have in your home or on a camping trip.

Most campsites have cooking areas provided where food can be safely cooked. Know fire restrictions when camping. In high fire danger areas, charcoal may be banned.

When cooking in wooded areas, be sure charcoals or campfire embers are completely out before leaving them. Charcoal can start a forest fire if not properly handled. (See section on disposing of charcoal.)

FIRST AID

Any product hot enough to cook food can cause injury or accident. It is always a good idea to have first aid supplies nearby in case of burns. If burned while cooking, cool the affected area with cold water as soon as possible or keep a first aid product, such as Burn Free®, available. Burn Free® is a jell that absorbs heat from a burn. It is the best first aid treatment for burns we have ever used. If burns are severe, seek medical attention as soon as possible.

Always be aware of the danger of fire when working with charcoal or any other heat source. Keep a safe distance from any flammable surfaces.

A WORD ABOUT STACKING OVENS

It is possible to stack several ovens using the top heat of one oven as the bottom heat for another. This is one way of reducing the amount of charcoal needed. We seldom stack ovens in regular cooking and never when the quality of food really matters.

Here's why:
The number of charcoal needed on the top of your oven and the number needed on the bottom are seldom the same. This will only be efficient if equal heat, top and bottom, is required.

Checking and rotating ovens is more difficult when the oven on the bottom is the one needing attention.

Ovens full of food are heavy and the constant stacking and unstacking can be hard on the back and very tiring.

CAMP CHEF PRODUCTS

Some of the products sold by Camp Chef are:
UDO® (Ultimate Dutch Oven®). This oven is available in 14-inch only.

All-Purpose Stove (APS)™. A new cooking appliance which uses charcoal for barbecuing, grilling or Dutch oven cooking. Designed for efficient charcoal use and has many other features.

5, 10, 12 and 14-inch Regular Dutch Oven.

10-inch and 13-inch skillets with lids. 'Comfort Gripper' handles are ergonomically designed.

Cast Iron Wok. Measures 13 inches in diameter with a flat bottom and has 'Comfort Gripper' handle.

ADO® - Aluminum version of the UDO® in 14-inch.

Accessory Pak. Includes aluminum griddle and a high rise lid, which is available for the UDO 14-inch and ADO 14-inch. This creates two pots and increases the capacity and versatility of both ovens.

Stoves. Low-pressure burners are best suited for Dutch oven cooking and are good for starting charcoal. They are available in 3-burner, 2-burner and 1-burner models.

High-pressure burners can be used for starting charcoal. They are best suited for deep frying, boiling and steaming where rapid heat recovery is important. They are available in 1-burner, 2-burner and mixed high- and low-pressure models.

Camp Table with Legs. A 14-inch x 32-inch steel table which allows Dutch oven cooking above ground. It comes equipped with leg extensions to change the cooking height and a three-sided windscreen. An optional shelf for holding cooking equipment is available. This heavy-duty table and can hold two Dutch ovens side by side and is sturdy enough to hold stacked ovens.

Camp Chef Cleaner and Conditioner®. See sections on Cleaning and Seasoning.

Lighter Basket. Used to start charcoal.

During the past two decades, Camp Chef has been the innovative leader in making products for those of us who like to "Live Outdoors." Their line of Dutch ovens is no exception.

For more information on

Camp Chef cast iron cookware,

visit www.campchef.com

OR

call 1-800-650-2433

The ADO® and UDO® have a unique design new to the Dutch Oven market. Both of these ovens have a cone built into the center of the pot that allows heat to radiate towards the outside, similar to using a Bundt pan.

Inside the oven are two racks for multi-level cooking. The lid also has legs and is deeper than a conventional Dutch oven lid. It can be used separately as a skillet over charcoal or propane.

Cooking techniques with these ovens over propane are slightly different than those used with charcoal. When using propane, it is best to use a low flame. Stir foods often if possible. When cooking meat, be sure to use the bottom rack and approximately two cups of liquid. This is especially true when using the aluminum oven.

When using charcoal with the ADO® and UDO®, it is not necessary to put a briquet in the middle of the cone area since the heat radiates towards the center.

With the hot air circulation in the ADO® and UDO®, food will cook faster. When cooking breads and cakes, be sure to rotate the pot and lid in opposite directions every 10 minutes.

When cooking roasts or chicken pieces, the lid can be used to brown the meat with one-fourth cup of oil. Place the lid over propane or briquets and pre-heat. When hot, add meat and brown all surfaces then transfer to the pot with bottom rack inserted. If using chicken pieces, they can be layered to fill the pot. Cook until the internal temperature of the meat meets USDA standards, see page 111.

If adding vegetables, leave enough room to add the top rack, add vegetables and cook until tender.

If cooking over an open fire, the smoke from the fire can enter the ADO® and UDO® through the holes in the cone. If smoke-flavored food is not desired, a piece of aluminum foil can be placed in the underside of the cone to block the smoke.

If smoke flavor is desired, use mesquite charcoal or wet wood chips to create smoke which will permeate the contents.

A whole chicken can be cooked by placing the chicken directly over the cone. Sprinkle with seasonings and cook until done.

RECIPES - BEGINNING

Flaky Baking Powder Biscuits, page 46

Beginners Cooking Tips

Breads
- Flaky Baking Powder Biscuits
- Basic Cornbread
- Prepared Frozen Rolls

Breakfast
- Breakfast Casserole

Main Dishes
- Fried Chicken
- Gerry's Stir Fry
- Barbecued Chicken or Ribs
- Sweet Chicken Delight
- All American Baked Beans
- Dutch Oven Potatoes
- Simple Roast

Desserts
- Black Forest Cobbler
- Peach Cobbler
- Apple Spice Cobbler

"This book is a road map that will guide you, from beginner to advanced, down the road of Dutch oven cooking — being led by an expert tour guide."

Dellis Hatch, Dutch oven expert

THE RECIPES

We have presented the basic principles for Dutch oven cooking in Part I. Now let's put them into practice.

The Beginning Section presents step by step instructions for those who have had little or no experience cooking in a Dutch oven.

The Intermediate Section is for those who are comfortable cooking in a Dutch oven but would like to fine-tune their skills.

The Advanced Section is for those who want to broaden their horizons. These recipes include additional techniques and garnishing tips. From here, the possibilities are limitless.

COOKING TIPS FOR BEGINNERS

Before beginning any cooking, review the selected recipe. Read through the instructions making sure each step is understood. Read through the ingredient list making sure all ingredients are available.

A common reason for recipe failure is leaving out or substituting an ingredient. Another reason is improper measuring of ingredients. Make sure all ingredients are measured accurately.

Using Aluminum Foil

Aluminum foil is an item every cook should have on hand. It can be used for so many different purposes, it is impossible to name them all. Some outdoor cooks like to line their ovens with foil for easy cleanup.

Here are some reasons why it is not necessary to line Dutch ovens:

If an oven is properly seasoned, it will have a smooth hard finish, which can be cleaned easily.

Cooking utensils can puncture the foil lining. If any foods or juices seep between the foil and the pot during cooking, it will be difficult to clean. This is especially a problem with sugar based desserts.

Our desire is to teach skills. These skills should make it possible to adapt recipes from any quality cookbook to Dutch oven use. Thus an extensive recipe section is not necessary.

Once assembly has begun, put items away as they are used. This helps to insure that an ingredient has not been left out and speeds up preparation.

Before doing any cooking, take time to level the cooking surface. If the surface is not level, breads, cakes and desserts will be lop-sided.

When baking cakes and breads, avoid lifting the lid for the first 20 minutes of cooking as this may cause them to fall. Also, for even heating, gently rotate the pot one-quarter turn every 15 minutes and rotate the lid one-quarter turn in the opposite direction.

If a food item needs to be removed for show, such as a pie or specialty bread, it is better to use parchment paper than foil. (See Advanced Section.)

Using Other Cookware

If concerned about cooking directly on the bottom of the oven, try using pizza pans, Bundt pans, cake pans, or pie plates (glass or metal) inside the Dutch oven. To allow airflow around the cookware, place coins, canning rings, racks, trivets, etc. beneath them.

Before placing other bakeware inside the Dutch oven, remember that it may have to be removed while the oven is hot. Make 'lifting strips' by tearing a piece of aluminum foil approximately two feet long in half lengthwise. Fold each length until approximately two inches wide. Lay the strips in an "X" pattern in the oven and place the cookware on the strips. Fold the top edges of the strips inside the oven so they do not interfere with the cooking food. Do not fold strips over the oven lip because the lid will not fit tightly and moisture will escape. When cooking is done and the food has slightly cooled, carefully lift items out of the oven with the foil strips. This usually takes two people.

Handling Baked Items

Soggy breads and desserts result when moisture is trapped inside a warm oven. To avoid this, remove the oven from the heat source and set lid ajar as soon as the baked goods are cooked. It is best to remove baked goods from the Dutch oven within 10-15 minutes after cooking to keep crusts crisp.

FLAKY BAKING POWDER BISCUITS

This basic Baking Powder Biscuit recipe can be used for many different purposes. Use it by itself for breakfast, as a topping over chili or stew (see Biscuit Topped Chili) or use a variation as a dessert. (See Intermediate Dessert Section, Fruit Roll-Ups.)

Step 1.   Gather ingredients.

Step 2.   Start at least 24 charcoal briquets using one of the methods listed in the Starting Charcoal Section.

Step 3.   In large bowl mix flour, cream of tartar, sugar, baking powder and salt. (Add 1/2 t. soda if using buttermilk.) With a pastry blender or two knives, cut the shortening into the dry ingredients. This is an important step. Take the time to blend the shortening in thoroughly. The mixture should have a course crumb texture. Set this mixture aside.

Step 4.   In a smaller bowl whisk together the egg and milk or buttermilk.

Step 5.   Using a spatula, carefully stir wet ingredients into dry ingredients until moist. Over-mixing will create a tough biscuit. Dough will be a little sticky.

Step 6.   Wipe a clean working surface with a dampened paper towel or clean moist cloth. While still damp, sprinkle an area approximately 12-inches x 18-inches with flour. Brush aside any flour that does not adhere to the moisture. Place dough onto floured surface and lightly sprinkle with flour.

Step 7.   Carefully fold dough from outside to center adding flour as necessary until dough is no longer sticky and can be rolled out. Avoid over-working as this too, will result in tough biscuits.

Step 8.   Roll dough to a thickness of 1/2-inch - 3/4-inch. Cut biscuits into circles approximately 21/2-inches in diameter. If a biscuit cutter is not available, use the rim of a glass or a small can with both ends removed. Thicker dough will produce fewer and taller biscuits, which will require longer cooking time. Thinner dough produces more...

You will need:

12" Dutch Oven

24 Charcoal Briquets

Makes Approximately
   12 Biscuits

3 1/2 cup flour

3/4 teaspoon cream of tartar

1 1/2 tablespoon sugar

1 1/2 tablespoon baking powder

1/2 tsp. salt

3/4 cup butter-flavored
   shortening

2 egg, beaten

2/3 cup milk
   (or buttermilk)

For Buttermilk Biscuits:

Substitute buttermilk for milk and add 1/2 teaspoon baking soda.

Beginning

For quick assembly when camping, pre-measure dry ingredients, cut in shortening and place in a Ziplock® bag. (Remember to store in a cool place.) When you get to camp, add wet ingredients right in the bag. Knead ingredients in the bag (remember over-mixing makes tough biscuits). Roll out and bake as directed.

biscuits with a crunchier crust and will require a shorter cooking time.

Step 9.   Lightly spray Dutch oven with spray oil or lightly grease with shortening. Arrange biscuits in the bottom of the oven. Cook with 8 charcoal briquets on the bottom and 16 on top for 20-30 minutes, depending on weather conditions and altitude, until browned.

Note: After 15 minutes of cooking, feel free to lift the lid and check the progress of the biscuits. Cook until golden brown on top and bottom. Biscuits can be gently lifted with a spatula to check the bottom.

Over-cooking produces dry biscuits.

BASIC CORNBREAD

Step 1. Gather ingredients.

Step 2. Start at least 24 charcoal briquets.

Step 3. In a medium bowl mix flour, cornmeal, baking powder and salt.

Step 4. In a small bowl mix sugar, egg, milk, (buttermilk), and oil.

Step 5. Make a well in the center of the dry ingredients and pour in the wet ingredients. With a spatula, gently stir just until moistened. Over-mixing will make the cornbread tough.

Step 6. Lightly coat bottom of Dutch oven with spray oil or lightly grease with shortening and pour in batter. Level with spatula.

Step 7. Bake with 8 briquets on the bottom and 16 on top for approximately 45 minutes.

Cook until toothpick inserted in the center comes out clean and bread pulls away from the sides of the oven. Serve with honey- butter or favorite jam.

Option: Substitute 1 cup of buttermilk for 1 cup of milk. Add 1/2 teaspoon of baking soda to dry ingredients.

HONEY BUTTER
Whip together:
1 part honey, 3 parts butter, pinch of cinnamon (optional)

You will need:

12" Dutch Oven

24 Charcoal Briquets

Serves 12-15

2 cups flour

2 cups cornmeal

2 tablespoons baking powder

1 teaspoon salt

1 cup sugar

4 eggs

1 cup buttermilk

1 3/4 cups milk

1/2 cup oil

When greasing pans for breads, only oil the bottom and about 1-inch up the sides. If the sides are oiled, the bread will climb the sides and slide back down as it cooks, leaving a crispy raised edge.

Beginning

PREPARED FROZEN ROLLS

Allow yeast breads to cook at least 15-20 minutes before checking to prevent falling. If rolls are browning too quickly, redistribute charcoal as necessary or rotate lid and pot more often to avoid hot spots. Too many rolls will cause dough to raise too high making the tops brown while the center is still doughy. Practice with frozen dough to achieve perfectly baked products.

Tips for Using Prepared Frozen Rolls.
(We Prefer Rhodes®)

Frozen dough will usually more than double in size. Follow manufacturer's instructions for thawing and raising. When using frozen dough, become familiar with the characteristics of the product. Allow plenty of room for expansion and raising.

In a 12-inch Dutch oven place 16 regular sized rolls. Allow rolls to rise until almost double and bake with 8 coals on the bottom and 16 on top for approximately 30 minutes. Rotate the pot and lid in opposite directions every 15 minutes. Rolls are done when golden brown on top, have pulled away from the sides of the oven and sound hollow when tapped.

If using larger rolls, leave a one-half inch space around each roll to allow for raising.

BREAKFAST CASSEROLE

Step 1.   Gather ingredients.

Step 2.   Brown sausage in Dutch oven. Add onions and garlic. Cook until onions are clear. Drain off any excess grease.

          Cover to keep warm.

Step 3.   In mixing bowl whisk eggs, mustard, salt and pepper until frothy.

Step 4.   Mix hashbrowns and sausage in the bottom of the Dutch oven. Using a spatula or the back of a spoon, smooth the top. Slowly pour eggs over potato-sausage mixture.

Step 5.   Bake with 8 charcoal on the bottom and 16 on top for 45-60 minutes until set. Sprinkle the cheese on top, let sit 5-10 minutes until cheese is melted. Serve with chili sauce or salsa, if desired.

You will need:

12" Dutch Oven

24 Charcoal Briquets

1 lb regular Pork sausage

1 medium onion, chopped

2 garlic cloves, chopped

12 eggs

1/2 teaspoon dry mustard

1/2 teaspoon salt

1/4 teaspoon pepper

2 lbs hashbrowns, frozen

2 cups cheese, grated

Serves 10-12

Ham, sausage links or bacon may be substituted for sausage.

Beginning

FRIED CHICKEN

You will need:

12" Dutch Oven

24 Charcoal Briquets

8 Chicken pieces of choice -
  boneless, skinless preferred

1 C. Flour (for coating)

1 tsp. Poultry Seasoning

1 Tbsp. Lowry® or
  Camp Chef® Seasoning Salt

1 Tbsp. Parsley Flakes
  (optional)

2 Eggs

Serves 8

Coating will adhere to chicken pieces better if refrigerated for at least one hour before cooking. Layer prepared pieces in a plastic container and cover.

If camping, this can be prepared at home and placed in Zip Lock® bags for storage in an ice chest. Best if used within 24 hours.

Steps one through six can be done in advance then refrigerate.

Step 1. Gather ingredients.

Step 2. Start at least 24 charcoal briquets.

Step 3. Rinse and drain chicken pieces.

Step 4. Whisk two eggs in a small shallow container. Set aside.

Step 5. Mix flour, poultry seasoning, seasoning salt and parsley flakes. Place in shallow dish. (A pie plate works well for this.)

Step 6. Dip chicken pieces in egg then dredge in flour mixture. Set aside until all pieces are coated. Optional: In a quart or gallon size Zip Lock® bag, combine dry ingredients. Shake to mix. After dipping chicken pieces in egg, place one or two pieces at a time in the bag and shake to coat.

Step 7. Place 12-14 charcoal briquets under the Dutch oven (or use propane stove). Heat 1/4 cup oil in oven or UDO® lid. When hot, brown chicken pieces on all sides. Note: Coating absorbs oil when browning. Add oil as necessary.

Step 8. (If using a UDO® lid, transfer chicken pieces to the bottom rack in the UDO® base.) When all pieces are browned, layer in bottom of Dutch oven. If available, place a rack or trivet in the bottom of the oven to keep chicken pieces out of drippings. This will also prevent over-cooking of bottom pieces when layering. Place the lid on the pot and remove all but 8 charcoal from under the oven. Add charcoal to the lid to total 16.

Step 9. Bake 45-60 minutes. Test for doneness with a thermometer. Boneless chicken should be 170°; bone-in should be 180°.

GERRY'S STIR FRY

Step 1.   Gather any of the ingredients in the amounts preferred according to availability. (This is a good recipe for using leftovers.) Chop or dice vegetables.

Step 2.   Cube meat and marinate in teriyaki sauce for a few hours.

Step 3.   Start 18-20 charcoal briquets or light propane stove and set to medium heat.

Step 4.   Heat 1/4 cup cooking oil in wok or Dutch oven. When oil is hot, stir in meat and cook until no longer pink. Add onion and garlic. Cook and stir until onions are clear. Add bouillon.

Step 5.   Add vegetables, stirring continually. When vegetables are tender add the spices and cashews. Stir.

Step 6.   When heated through, serve immediately.

Serve over rice or noodles. (If using Top Ramen® noodles, use the flavor packet in place of some of the spices.)

You will need:

12" Dutch Oven

18 - 20 Charcoal Briquets (bottom heat only)

OR

Wok over propane stove

OR

All-Purpose Stove (APS)™

Chicken, Pork or Beef

Broccoli, Celery, Cauliflower

Onions, Red or Green Pepper

Carrots, Snow Peas

Water Chestnuts, Cashews

Garlic, Mushrooms

Sesame Seeds, Bean sprouts

Seasonings:

1 teaspoon chicken bouillon, dissolved in 1 cup water

1/2 teaspoon ginger

1 tablespoon Teriyaki Sauce

1/2 teaspoon black pepper Lowry® or Camp Chef® Seasoning Salt

BARBECUED CHICKEN OR RIBS

You will need:

3-5 lbs of Chicken or Ribs

32 oz. catsup

1/2 cup brown sugar, packed

1 medium onion, chopped

1 green pepper, chopped

1 teaspoon salt

Dash Worcestershire Sauce

12 oz. Pepsi®

1 garlic clove

Dash Tabasco Sauce
  (optional)

Step 1. Combine ingredients for sauce.

Step 2. Start 10-12 charcoal briquets or light propane stove and set to medium heat. Adjust to simmer.

Step 3. Meat: Parboil (simmer in water to remove excess fats) for 15-20 minutes until no longer pink. Drain. Place in Dutch oven and cover with sauce. With lid ajar, simmer until tender, about 1 hour for chicken, 1 1/2 - 2 hours for ribs. (The longer these simmer, the better they get.)

SWEET CHICKEN DELIGHT

You will need:

1 20 oz. can Pineapple tidbits-
  save juice and add water to
  make 1 1/4 cup liquid

2/3 cup brown sugar, packed

1 garlic clove, minced

2 cup catsup

1 onion, chopped

3 Tablespoon vinegar

Dash Teriyaki Sauce

1 Chicken, cut in pieces

OR

6-8 Chicken breasts,
  boneless, skinless

Step 1. Gather ingredients.

Step 2. Start charcoal briquets or light propane stove and set to medium heat. Adjust as necessary.

Step 3. Combine all ingredients for sauce.

Step 4. Brown chicken pieces. Pour sauce over chicken. With lid ajar, simmer approximately 1 hour or until chicken is tender.

ALL-AMERICAN BAKED BEANS

Step 1. Gather ingredients.

Step 2. Start 12-14 charcoal briquets.

Step 3. When charcoal is hot, place Dutch oven over charcoal. Preheat oven for browning meats. Brown bacon and sausage. Remove grease and add vegetables; sauté until tender. Add all remaining ingredients.

Step 4. Simmer, stirring occasionally, with 8 briquets on the bottom, for 1 1/2-2 hours. Add more charcoal approximately 45 minutes into the cooking time. (When adding fresh charcoal, remove all ashes.)

You will need:

12-inch Dutch Oven

10 Charcoal Briquets
(bottom heat only)

OR

Propane Stove on low heat.

12 slices bacon, cut in to
1" pieces

1 green pepper, chopped

2 pounds sausage

2 medium onions, chopped

2 garlic cloves, minced

4 cans pork and beans
(21 oz.)

1 cup brown sugar, packed

1/4 cup Dijon mustard

1 C. Homestyle® Chili Sauce

2 Tbsp. Worcestershire Sauce

1/2 tsp. Tabasco Sauce (optional)

Serves 12-15

Beginning

DUTCH OVEN POTATOES

You will need:

12" Dutch Oven

24 Charcoal Briquets

1 pound bacon, cut in to
1" pieces

12-14 medium potatoes,
peeled and sliced

2 onions, diced

1 garlic clove, minced

1 pound cheddar cheese,
shredded

Salt and Pepper

OR

Camp Chef Seasoning Salt
to taste

Green or Red Peppers,
(optional)

Serves 10-12

To keep potatoes from turning
brown, place in cold water
immediately after slicing. Rinse
several times until all starch is
removed. Store in cold water
until just before cooking.
Drain and use as directed.

Step 1. Gather ingredients. Ham, sausage, or hamburger
can be substituted for bacon. Frozen potatoes
can be substituted for fresh.

Step 2. Start at least 24 charcoal briquets.

Step 3. Brown bacon. Remove all but 3 tablespoons of
bacon grease from the oven. Add onions and
garlic. Sauté until onions are clear.

Step 4, Add potatoes. Season and stir.

Step 5. Bake for 25 minutes with 8 charcoal on the
bottom and 16 on top. Taste potatoes and add
seasoning, if necessary. Stir approximately one-
half of the cheese into the potatoes. Cover and
continue to cook.

Step 6. Bake 45-60 minutes or until tender. Taste one
more time for proper seasoning. Add salt and
pepper or seasoning salt if necessary. Add
remaining cheese to top only. Replace lid and
continue cooking until cheese is melted.

SIMPLE ROAST

Step 1. Gather ingredients.

Step 2. Start charcoal briquets or light propane stove to medium heat to brown.

Step 3. Heat Dutch oven or UDO® lid. Pour in 1/4 cup oil and brown meat on all sides. If cooking in regular Dutch oven, put roast on a rack or trivet. If using a UDO®, place meat on bottom rack.

Step 4. Add 1 cup water. Sprinkle dry onion soup mix on top of roast.

Step 5. Roasts are better slow simmered. Reduce propane stove to simmer. Roast with 10 charcoal briquets on bottom and 10 on the top for approximately 1 1/2 hours. Replace charcoal after 45 minutes.

Step 6. If using a UDO®, place top rack in oven and layer vegetables on rack. In a regular Dutch oven, arrange vegetables around meat.

Step 7. Cook until vegetables are tender and meat reaches correct temperatures (see Food Safety Section). Let meat rest 10 minutes before carving. Season vegetables before serving.

You will need:

12" Dutch Oven
OR UDO®
20 Charcoal Briquets

3-5 lb roast of choice
 (bone-in or boneless)

1 package dry onion
 soup mix

1 onion, sliced

6-8 red potatoes, washed
 and quartered

1 lb baby carrots

Salt and Pepper to taste

Serves 4-6

COBBLERS

When baking cobblers, rotate the lid and pot one quarter turn in opposite directions every 15 minutes

Serve cobblers with ice cream or whipped cream.

Cobblers are done when the top is golden brown, sides are slightly pulled away from the edges and a toothpick inserted in the cake comes out clean.

Loosely defined, a cobbler is a fruit dessert with a cake or biscuit-type topping. There are hundreds of variations. This is usually the first dish a new cook attempts because they are easy and taste so good.

Note: For the following cobbler recipes, mixing the cake mix according to directions instead of using soda is an option. It is also acceptable to use different combinations of cake mixes and fruit.

Variations
Cobblers are very forgiving. It rarely matters if the fruit or the batter is placed in the oven first. Texture of the batter is not compromised whether mixed as directed or using soda pop. Measurements do not need to be exact. Feel free to experiment with your favorite combinations of fruit and batters and sodas.

Try these ideas
Put pie fillings in the bottom. Sprinkle cake mix dry on top. Dot with 1/4 pound of butter.

Use Bisquick® mixed as directed by manufacturer in place of cake mix.

Top with Rhodes® frozen biscuits or homemade biscuits (see Crown Cobbler in Intermediate recipe section).

Spread pie filling in the bottom of the oven. Sprinkle dry cake mix on pie filling and pour 1 can soda on top.

BLACK FOREST COBBLER

Step 1.   Gather ingredients.

Step 2.   Start at least 24 charcoal briquets.

Step 3.   In a large bowl, empty contents of cake mix. Pour soda into cake mix a little at a time, stirring after each addition until it reaches cake batter consistency.

Step 4.   Lightly spray Dutch oven with spray oil. Empty contents of pie filling into oven. Distribute evenly with a spatula.

Step 5.   Gently pour batter over pie filling. Spread evenly.

Step 6.   Bake with 8 charcoal briquets on the bottom and 16 on the top for 45-60 minutes or until done.

You will need:

12" Dutch Oven

24 Charcoal Briquets

29 oz.can cherry pie filling

1 devil's food cake mix

12-16 ozs. cream soda

OR

Lemon-lime soda

Serves 12-15

PEACH COBBLER

You will need:

29 oz. can sliced peaches in syrup

1 yellow or white cake mix

12-16 ozs. cream soda

OR

Lemon-lime soda

Step 1. Gather ingredients.

Step 2. Start at least 24 charcoal briquets.

Step 3. Spray Dutch oven with non-stick oil or lightly grease with shortening.

Step 4. In a large bowl, empty contents of cake mix. Add soda a little at a time, stirring with each addition, until it reaches cake batter consistency. If batter seems too thick, add more soda pop to thin.

Step 5. Pour the mix in the Dutch oven.

Step 6. Spoon peaches on top of the cake mix, including the syrup.

Step 7. Bake with 8 charcoal briquets on the bottom and 16 on the top for 45-60 minutes or until done.

APPLE SPICE COBBLER

You will need:

1 spice cake mix

29 oz can apple pie filling

12-16 ounces cream soda

OR

Lemon-lime soda

Step 1. Gather ingredients.

Step 2. Start at least 24 charcoal briquets.

Step 3. In a large bowl, empty contents of cake mix. Add soda a little at a time, mixing after each addition until it reaches cake batter consistency.

Step 4. Spray Dutch oven with spray oil or lightly grease with shortening. Spread pie filling evenly across the bottom of the Dutch oven.

Step 5. Spread cake batter evenly over top.

Step 6. Bake 45-60 minutes or until done with 8 charcoal on the bottom and 16 on top.

RECIPES - INTERMEDIATE

Marie's Fabulous French Rolls, page 66

Intermediate Cooking Tips

Breads
- Dinner Rolls
- Apple Sauce Bread
- Marie's Fabulous French Rolls

Breakfast
- Egg Soufflé

Main Dishes
- Biscuit-topped Chili
- Grandma's Great Potatoes
- More than Taco Soup

Desserts
- Coconut Brownie
- Crown Cobbler
- Favorite Fruit Roll
- Almost Pumpkin Pie

Crown Cobbler, page 71 and Grandma's Great Potatoes, page 69

INTERMEDIATE COOKING TIPS

At this point we're assuming basic skills have been mastered and intimidation is gone. Let's dig in to some solid Dutch oven cooking. Having access to more than one Dutch oven will allow greater flexibility in the meals that can be created.

Cooking with yeast
This section introduces yeast rise breads, which many Dutch oven cooks avoid. Practice with these recipes. Confidence will grow with each success.

Yeast has been used in baked goods for centuries. It is a skill and an art. When making breads, certain steps must be taken to insure satisfactory results.

When a recipe gives a range for flour amounts, start with the minimum. For example: 6-8 cups flour. The exact amount of flour required can vary on any given day depending on altitude, humidity, type of flour, etc. Begin with 6 cups and add flour as necessary to keep the dough from becoming too dry.

Types of yeast – There are several different kinds of yeast. Rather than discuss all of them, we recommend using active dry yeast. We prefer SAF® Instant, which can be added to dry ingredients without activating first. Pre-measured packets of other brands are available which contain 1 tablespoon of yeast. Using quick-rising yeast will decrease rising time by about one-third.

Making dough with water for the liquid will make a crisper crust. Making dough with milk for the liquid will make a softer crust. To insure proper yeast activation, liquids should be 115°-120°.

If yeast is questionable (past the expiration date), place a small amount in warm sugar water. If it bubbles, it is still active.

The best temperature for raising dough is 80°-85°.

Allow time for yeast to work.

Follow the recipe closely when making yeast breads.

To determine when dough is ready to bake, press with a finger until it leaves an impression. If the impression remains, the dough is ready.

Bread will rise more rapidly at high altitudes.

The best way to recognize good dough is by touch. During kneading, the feel of the dough determines whether more flour should be added. If dough is sticky and difficult to work add flour a little at a time. Work in flour after each addition until dough becomes smooth and elastic with a satin sheen.

Intermediate

If dough is not rising quickly enough, add 4 charcoal briquets to the lid only. This provides the warmth needed by the yeast. Once charcoal has been placed on the lid, watch closely to avoid over-rising of the dough.

On a hot summer day, a black Dutch oven can be extremely warm when placed in the sun. To avoid killing yeast, keep ovens in the shade. On cold winter days, use sunshine to your advantage by placing the Dutch oven in the sun.

Experiment with herbs and spices. Learn to use fresh as well as dried. Use 2 tablespoons fresh herbs to 1 teaspoon dried.

Begin cooking before dough is fully doubled. Dough continues to rise during baking.

Bread is done when sides are pulled away from the pot and bread sounds hollow when tapped.

Brushing crusts with butter after baking will create a soft shiny crust. Brushing crusts with milk, water or beaten egg before baking will produce a crispy crust.

Try kneading bread on an oiled surface instead of a floured surface. This produces a shiny soft dough and keeps dough from sticking to hands and counter top.

Adapting recipes to taste

We have just said to follow recipes closely when working with breads. Now we are going to encourage creativity with other recipes.

Keep a pencil with your cookbook and record each time a recipe is used. What did you like about the recipe? What would you change? When a recipe becomes a favorite, make a copy and keep it in an organized file. We have three 3-ring binders - one for main dishes, one for sides and one for desserts.

When altering recipes, keep a record of each change so it can be duplicated in the future.

Creating complete meals

Cooking one pot of food is an achievement. Preparing an entire meal is an even greater accomplishment. Preparing several dishes and having them ready at the same time takes planning and organization.

Try selecting three recipes from this book - a main dish, bread and dessert. After choosing the recipes, write approximate preparation and cooking times for each recipe. Create a timetable working back from the serving time. Allow extra time for unexpected interruptions or setbacks. Make sure hot foods will be served hot. If there are helpers, one person should be in charge and assign responsibilities so that preparation and cooking run smoothly. Be sure to plan for non-food preparations like setting tables, drinks and cleanup.

DINNER ROLLS

- Mix yeast, water, and a pinch of sugar and set aside.
- Bring milk and butter to a boil and cool to lukewarm. Add yeast mixture, egg, sugar, and salt. Add flour to make soft dough (approx. 3 cups) and let rise.
- Shape rolls into desired shapes (for uniform roll sizes see Advanced Breads section), let rise.
- Brush with melted butter and bake with 8 charcoal briquets on the bottom and 16 on the top for 20-30 minutes or until golden brown.

You will need:

12" Dutch Oven

24 Charcoal Briquets

1 packet dry yeast

1 1/3 Tbsp. warm water

2 cups milk

3 tablespoons butter

1 egg

1/3 cup sugar

1 teaspoon salt

3-4 cups flour

2 Tbsp. butter, softened

Serves 24

1 1/4 ounce. package of active dry yeast is equal to a scant tablespoon of yeast.

Intermediate

APPLESAUCE BREAD

You will need:

12" Dutch Oven

24 Charcoal Briquets

1/2 cup vegetable oil

1 15 oz.can applesauce,
   unsweetened

2 cups sugar

2 eggs, whole

1 teaspoon vanilla

4 cups flour

1 teaspoon baking powder

2 teaspoon baking soda

1 teaspoon.salt

1/3 cup milk

1/2 teaspoon nutmeg

1 teaspoon cinnamon

1/2 cup walnuts, chopped

2 Tbsp. grated lemon

OR

Orange rind

Topping

1/2 cup brown sugar

1/4 teaspoon cinnamon

1/4 cup walnuts, chopped

Serves 8-10

- Lightly spray Dutch oven with spray oil.
- In a large bowl, combine oil, applesauce, granulated sugar, eggs and vanilla.
- In a separate bowl, combine flour, baking powder, baking soda, salt, orange rind, and spices. Stir in nuts.
- Add flour mixture to applesauce mixture alternating with milk.
- Mix until ingredients are thoroughly moistened. Pour batter into prepared oven. Mix topping ingredients and sprinkle on top of batter.
- Bake approximately for an hour or until toothpick inserted in the center comes out clean.
- Remove from Dutch oven and place on rack to cool.

MARIE'S FABULOUS FRENCH ROLLS

- Mix one-half cup lukewarm water with yeast and sugar in a separate bowl to dissolve. Set aside and let activate.
- Add salt and butter to 1 cup hot water.
- In a large mixing bowl, combine hot water mixture and 2 cups flour. Beat until well blended.
- Add yeast mixture and 1 cup flour and mix. Add another cup of flour. Blend. Add more flour if necessary to make moderately stiff dough. Knead until satiny and well mixed. Let rise for one-half hour.
- Punch dough down and form into balls. Dip balls into melted butter and place in a 12-inch Dutch oven. Sprinkle with sesame seeds.
- Cover and allow to rise until doubled in size.
- Bake with 6-8 coals on the bottom and about 16 on top. Rotate pot one-quarter turn every 5 minutes and lid in opposite direction.
- Butter the tops of the rolls when they are golden brown and serve with butter, honey or jam. This recipe makes 12 rolls.

You will need:

12" Dutch Oven

24 Charcoal Briquets

1/2 cup lukewarm water

2 teaspoons yeast

1 tablespoon sugar

1 cup hot water

1 teaspoon salt

2 tablespoons butter

4 cups flour

12 Servings

This recipe comes from Craig and Marie Ruesch.

It is one of our favorites.

For uniform roll size, see Advanced Breads section.

Intermediate

EGG SOUFFLÉ

You will need:

12" Dutch Oven
24 Charcoal Briquets

18 eggs
1 pound country sausage
1 medium onion, diced
1 4 oz. can chopped green chilies
15 slices of bread
Salt and Pepper to taste
1/2 pound cheddar cheese,
   shredded
1 green onion, chopped
   (optional)
Sliced olives (optional)

Serves 10-12

Here's a breakfast recipe you're
sure to enjoy from Dellis and
Delores Hatch.

• Brown sausage, onions, and green chilies. Remove and discard crust from bread. Cut bread into one-inch squares.

• Crack eggs into a large mixing bowl and beat well. Salt and pepper to taste.

• Spray a 12-inch Dutch oven with oil.

• Add sausage mixture and bread cubes. Pour eggs over sausage and bread. Gently stir eggs, bread and sausage until bread is thoroughly coated.

• Bake with 8 charcoal on the bottom and 16 on top bake for one hour or until eggs are firm to the touch. Carefully rotate the lid one-quarter turn every 15 minutes and rotate pot in opposite direction to avoid hot spots. Jarring the oven could cause the soufflé to fall.

• Sprinkle with shredded cheese, green onion pieces, or olive slices. Serve with salsa.

BISCUIT-TOPPED CHILI

For Biscuits:
- Use the biscuit recipe on page 44 EXCEPT add 1 cup shredded cheese to the dry ingredients before adding wet ingredients.
- In Dutch oven brown meat. Add onion, pepper and garlic and sauté until onion is clear. Add remaining ingredients. Bring to a boil.
- Reduce heat to simmer and place biscuits on top. Place 18 briquets on top to brown biscuits. Continue simmering 45-50 minutes until biscuits are brown. If biscuits are not browning as desired, place lid ajar for some of the moisture to escape and continue cooking.

You will need:

14" OR 12" Deep Dutch Oven

28 Charcoal Briquets

Serves 15-18

For Chili:
1 pound ground beef

OR

Pork sausage

1 onion, chopped

2 garlic cloves, minced

1 green pepper, chopped

1 32 oz. can stewed tomatoes

1 16 oz. can tomato sauce

1 15 1/4 oz. can whole
       kernel corn

5 Tbsp. Worcestershire Sauce

3 tsp. oregano

4 tsp. chili powder

1 tsp. Tabasco Sauce

1 32 oz. can ted beans, drained
and rinsed

Intermediate

GRANDMA'S GREAT POTATOES

You will need:

6-8 medium potatoes

1 garlic clove, minced

1 pint sour cream

1 teaspoon salt

10 ounce cheddar cheese,

1/8 teaspoon pepper

1 bunch green onions

2 tablespoons melted butter

3 tablespoons milk

1/3 cup stuffing mix crumbs

- Cook, peel and grate potatoes.
- Add sour cream, grated cheese, chopped onions and garlic.
- Add milk, salt and pepper stirring to distribute throughout potatoes.
- Press into oven, smoothing top.
- Stir butter into crumbs and sprinkle on top.
- Bake with 8 coals on the bottom and 14-16 on top for 35-45 minutes.
- This recipe has been a family favorite for years.
- Serves 10-12

MORE THAN TACO SOUP

You will need:

1 pound lean ground beef

1 medium onion, chopped

2 garlic cloves, chopped

8 ounces tomato sauce

4 ounces green chilies

15 1/4 oz. can kidney beans

15 1/4 oz. can whole kernel corn

14 1/2 oz. can stewed tomatoes, Mexican style

1 1 1/4 oz. package Lowry's Taco Seasoning®

1 tsp. Worcestershire Sauce

1/2 tsp. Jalapeno Tabasco Sauce (add more if desired)

1 10 oz. can enchilada sauce

2-3 C. shredded cabbage

- Brown ground beef.
- Add onion and garlic and sauté until onion is clear.
- Combine all ingredients and simmer 30 minutes with 12 charcoal briquets on the bottom.
- Serves 6-8

COCONUT BROWNIE

- Mix cake mix, butter and egg. This will make a stiff batter.
- Spray a 12-inch Dutch oven with spray oil and spread batter in bottom of oven.
- Combine remaining ingredients and spread over Devil's Food mixture.
- Bake 35-40 minutes with 8 charcoal briquets on the bottom and 16 on the top or until toothpick inserted in the center pulls out clean and brownie has pulled away from sides of the oven. Like any brownie dessert, this will be very moist.
- Do not over-bake.

You will need:

12" Dutch Oven

24 Charcoal Briquets

1 Devil's food cake mix

$1/2$ cup butter, melted

1 egg

$1 1/2$ cup coconut

1 egg

14 oz. can sweetened condensed milk

$2/3$ cup walnuts

10 maraschino cherries, diced or chopped

$1/4$ cup maraschino cherry juice

4 tablespoons flour

Serves 18-20

Intermediate

CROWN COBBLER

You will need:

12" Dutch Oven

24 Charcoal Briquets

16 regular Rhodes® rolls cut in half

1 teaspoon almond flavoring

2-21 oz. cans cherry pie filling

1/2 cup butter, melted

Zest of one orange

3/4 cup sugar

1 teaspoon cinnamon

Serves 12-15

This is the King of Cobblers!

- Combine almond flavoring and pie filling. Spread in the bottom of the oven.
- Combine orange zest, sugar and cinnamon.
- Roll each piece of dough in butter then in orange/sugar/cinnamon mixture. Arrange rolls in the bottom of the Dutch oven, spacing evenly. Rolls will not be touching. Let rise until double.
- Cook with 8 coals on the bottom and 16 on top for 45-55 minutes or until rolls are golden brown and have pulled away from the sides of the oven.

NOTE: If rolls are rising too slowly, place 4-6 hot charcoal briquets on the lid.

If desired, make a glaze with 1 cup of powdered sugar and 1 tablespoon of milk to drizzle over rolls when slightly cooled.

FAVORITE FRUIT ROLL

- Mix flour, sugar, baking powder and salt. Cut in shortening and add milk.
- On a floured surface, roll into a rectangle approximately 12-inches x 18-inches. Top with grated apples and lightly sprinkle with cinnamon.
- Starting with a long side, roll up in jellyroll fashion and cut into 12 equal rolls. Use dental floss or string to score and cut the rolls. The apples contain a lot of juice, rolls will be very moist. Work quickly.

Syrup:
- Bring syrup ingredients to a boil and remove from heat. Gently arrange rolls in hot syrup leaving space between rolls for expansion.
- Bake with 8 charcoal on the bottom and 18 on top (375º) for 20-25 minutes. Dessert is done when rolls have expanded to fill the entire oven bottom and are golden brown.

You will need:

12" Dutch Oven

24 Charcoal Briquets

3 cups flour

3 tablespoons sugar

4 teaspoons baking powder

1 teaspoon salt

1/2 cup shortening

1 1/4 cups milk

5-6 medium apples making 3 cups grated

Sprinkle with cinnamon

Serves 12

Intermediate

Syrup
1 1/2 cups sugar

2 cups water

5 drops red food coloring (optional)

This recipe is always a hit when we cook it for friends and family.

It's very impressive and oh so good.

Top with a scoop of vanilla ice cream.

ALMOST PUMPKIN PIE

You will need:

12" Dutch Oven
24 Charcoal Briquets

Filling:

1 29 oz. can pumpkin
3 tsp. pumpkin pie spice
3 eggs
1 cup sugar
1/2 teaspoon salt
1 teaspoon vanilla
1 cup evaporated milk

Topping:

1 package yellow cake mix
1 cup chopped pecans
1 cup butter

Serves 12-15

While still warm, serve with whipped cream or ice cream.

- Mix all filling ingredients. Pour into a greased 12-inch Dutch oven.
- Cut butter into cake mix with a pastry blender, then mix in nuts. Sprinkle over top of filling.
- Bake for 1 hour with 8 charcoal on the bottom and 16 on top.
- Dessert is done when a knife inserted in the center comes out clean.
- Serve warm or cold.

RECIPES - ADVANCED

Encore Fudge Cake, page 87

Advanced Cooking Tips

Breads
- Uniform Rolls
- Kaiser Rolls
- Butterhorns
- Parker House Rolls
- Best Ever Cinnamon Rolls

Main Dishes
- Savory Stuffed Pork Roast
- Golden Cashew Chicken
- State Fair Chili

Desserts
- Perfect Pecan Cake
- Apple Crumb Pie
- Encore Fudge Cake

Garnishing

Cooking for Crowds

Apple Crumb Pie, page 86; Butterhorn Rolls, page 80; Golden Chicken Cashew, page 83;

ADVANCED COOKING TIPS

Basic skills have now been mastered. Breads turn out golden brown top and bottom, meats are tender and cooked to perfection and desserts are delightful. Failures come less often (everybody has them) and it's time to tackle the challenges. Now the "sky's the limit."

We are including a few suggestions for some advanced recipes but there are thousands of cookbooks, magazines and newspaper articles with recipes just waiting to be cooked. Use your imagination and creativity. Take pictures and keep a scrapbook if you like. Try cooking in a Cook-off. Don't be afraid to venture outside your comfort zone.

Parchment Paper
Parchment paper is an essential cooking tool for the experienced Dutch oven cook. For breads with sweet fillings, pies and other desserts that need to be removed from the oven before serving, this paper is a must.

It can also be used to wrap roasts to maintain moisture during roasting.

Spray the inside of the Dutch oven with a light coat of spray oil. Cut the parchment paper into the necessary shape and place it in the oven. Spray a light coating of spray oil on the parchment paper, then place the food in the oven.

After the food is cooked and slightly cooled, remove the food from the oven as directed on page 77 and gently peel away the parchment paper. Voila! You have a winner!

When removing pies or delicate pastries for presentation, use parchment paper strips to lift food out of the oven. Inverting can damage delicate crusts.

Advanced

These methods work well for breads and cakes.

Inverting an oven

Occasionally baked goods need to be removed from the oven for presentation. This is especially important during competition. This requires teamwork. Here are two methods.

When removing pies or delicate pastries for presentation, use parchment paper strips to lift food out of the oven. Inverting can damage delicate crusts.

(1) Make a cardboard round slightly smaller than the diameter of the oven. It should drop down inside the Dutch oven and rest on the food. Cover the round with foil. After food is baked and slightly cooled, place round on top of food.

Person One: Using hot pads or oven mitts, grasp the ears of the pot (where the bale connects) making sure the bail is secure. With thumbs pointing away, lift oven up, tip the oven upside down and allow food to drop onto the round.

Person Two: Using hot pads or oven mitts, lift Dutch oven off food. As oven is being lifted, person one slides hands to center to steady round and food.

If presenting on an oven lid, make another round, slightly smaller than the diameter of the food being shown. Cover with foil. Center the second round on top of the food (which is actually the bottom of the food). Gently rotate hands and turn over oven until food is right side up. Place the smaller cardboard round and the food centered on an inverted Dutch oven lid. Place the lid on a lid stand.

NOTE: The purpose of the second cardboard round is to keep baked goods from following the contour of the oven lid and sinking in the center.

(2) Invert a tray or pizza pan over the opening of the Dutch oven. Using oven mitts or hot pads, grasp the ears of the pot and the edge of the tray or pan. With thumbs pointing away, hold tray to pot securely. Turn Dutch oven upside down and allow food to drop. When food has dropped, have another person lift the oven off the tray. Be sure to protect hands with gloves or hot pads.

If presenting on a tray, use a second tray to invert again. If presenting on a Dutch oven lid, use procedure in method one.

Both methods require practice and patience. With experimentation, teams may find other ways that work best for them.

Other Bakeware

It usually takes more skill to cook items directly on the bottom of a Dutch oven than using other bakeware. For example: a two-layer cake can be cooked in cake pans or in two 10-inch Dutch ovens. Greater skill is needed to cook in the two ovens and produce a beautiful layer cake.

There are times, however, when there are no alternatives, like using a Bundt pan. When it is necessary to use other bakeware in a Dutch oven, be sure that bakeware is thoroughly greased and floured so food will come out easily.

Remember that other bakeware will have to be removed when it is hot so devise a method for easy removal. (See sections on aluminum foil and parchment paper.)

BREADS

Uniform Rolls
Kaiser Rolls
Butterhorns
Parker House Rolls

Use a favorite dinner roll recipe to experiment with different roll shapes, or try these shapes with the dinner roll recipe found on pages 64 and 66.

Uniform Rolls
• Pinch off a piece of dough about 2-inches in diameter.

• Wrap fingers around the dough. Look at the distance between the ends of the fingers and the heel of the hand.

• Shape the dough into a ball and place in lightly oiled Dutch oven.

• Pinch off the next piece of dough and make sure it fits in the palm the same as the first roll. If it is a larger piece of dough, pinch off the excess. If it is smaller, add more.

• Make remaining rolls exactly the same size. After a batch or two of rolls, this will be easy and rolls will be uniform.

Kaiser Rolls
• Divide dough into 16-20 pieces.

• Roll each piece of dough into a rope 12-inches long.

• Crossing ends right over left, tie a loose knot in the center. Tuck one end into the top and one in the bottom.

• Place 2 to 3-inches apart in Dutch oven. Let rise and bake.

BREADS

Butterhorns

- Divide dough in half.
- Roll each half into a 12-inch circle. Brush with melted butter.
- With a pizza cutter, cut each circle into 12 wedges.
- Beginning at the outside edge, roll each wedge to the center. Place 2 to 3 inches apart in Dutch oven.
- Let rise and bake.

Parker House Rolls

- Roll dough to $1/4$-inch thick.
- Cut into $2 1/2$-inches circle. Brush with melted butter.
- Make an off-center crease with a butter knife. Fold larger half over smaller half.
- Place 2-inches apart in Dutch oven.
- Let rise and bake.

Advanced

BEST EVER CINNAMON ROLLS

You will need:

12" Dutch Oven
Approximately 12 large rolls
18-20 Charcoal Briquets

1 envelope dry yeast
2 tablespoon warm water
Pinch of sugar
2 cups milk
4 tablespoons butter
1 egg
3/4 cup sugar
3/4 teaspoon salt
6-8 cups flour
1 -2 teaspoons cinnamon
1/2 cup sugar
1/4 -1/2 cup walnuts
OR Pecans, chopped

Glaze:
6 tablespoons butter
2 cups powdered sugar
1 teaspoon vanilla
1 teaspoon almond flavoring
milk

These are prize-winning rolls.

The best way to cut cinnamon rolls is using thread or dental floss. A knife will flatten the dough instead of a making a nice crisp cut. After dough is rolled jellyroll style, cut a piece of dental floss or thread about 18-inches long. Lightly score the top of the dough to divide into equal sections. (Cutting off the ends will create more uniform rolls.) Slide the dental floss or thread under the dough, cross on top and pull. Floss will cut through the dough leaving a clean edge.

- Mix yeast, water and a pinch of sugar and set aside to work.
- In a small pan, bring milk and butter to a boil then cool to luke warm.
- When cool, add the yeast mixture, egg, sugar and salt.
- Add enough flour to make soft dough. Let rise.
- Roll dough into a 12-inch x 18-inch rectangle about 1/2-inch thick. Spread with butter and sprinkle with cinnamon, sugar and chopped nuts.
- From longest side, roll jellyroll fashion and cut into 12 rolls about 11/2-inches thick. Arrange in Dutch oven. Press with heel of hand to flatten a little so all rolls will raise the same.
- Let raise and bake 45-50 minutes with 12-14 coals on top and 6 on the bottom.

Glaze:
- Mix all ingredients adding only enough milk to give desired spreading consistency. Spread on rolls while still warm but not hot.
- Sprinkle with remaining nuts or other garnishing.

SAVORY STUFFED PORK ROAST

- Select a 3-3¹/2-pound boneless pork loin roast. Cut in half and then cut through the middle of each half lengthwise two-thirds of the way through. Set aside.
- Sauté the ingredients listed. Add spices to taste.
- Fill slits in loin halves with mixture and sandwich remaining mixture between the two halves. Tie securely.
- Rub outside surfaces of meat with a mixture of: 1 tablespoon fennel seed, crushed 2 teaspoons lemon pepper
- Wrap entire roast with 3-4 strips of bacon and secure with wooden picks.
- Wrap in parchment paper and place on rack. Cook 1 hour on medium heat then reduce heat and continue cooking until meat thermometer registers 155°-160°. Let meat rest 10-15 minutes and serve.

You will need:

12" Dutch Oven

24 Charcoal Briquets

3-3¹/2 lb pork loin roast, boneless

1 Tbsp. fennel seed, crushed
2 teaspoon lemon pepper

3-4 strips of bacon

Sauté:
1 tablespoon butter
¹/3 cup sweet red pepper, chopped

¹/3 cup sweet green pepper, chopped

¹/2 cup onion, finely chopped

2 garlic cloves, diced

¹/2 cup celery, chopped

Stir in:
1¹/2 teaspoons dried thyme, crushed

¹/4 tsp. ground red pepper

¹/2 teaspoon salt

¹/2 teaspoon paprika

Serves 6-8

GOLDEN CASHEW CHICKEN

You will need:

12" Dutch Oven

24 Charcoal Briquets

5 boneless, skinless chicken
   breast halves

Marinade:
1 part Teriyaki Sauce
2 parts lemon-lime soda
1/4 teaspoon horseradish
1/4 teaspoon garlic powder

Creamy Cheese Sauce:
8 ounces cream cheese
1 cup milk
pinch of garlic powder
1/4 cup Parmesan cheese grated

OR

1 garlic clove

Coating:
1 egg
2 cups stuffing mix crumbs
Paprika

Finely Chopped Vegetables:
1/4 cup broccoli, cauliflower
1 carrot
2 green onions,
2 tablespoons green pepper,
1 garlic clove
1/2-1 cup cashews

- Flatten chicken pieces between two layers of plastic wrap to 1/2-inch thick.
- Marinate 1-2 hours.
- To make cheese sauce: On low heat, melt cream cheese adding about 1/4 cup milk and garlic powder. Whisk to a smooth consistency then add Parmesan cheese to melt.
- Grate or chop vegetables. Sauté in small amount of butter just until tender then mix with 1/4 cup Creamy Cheese Sauce to make a paste. (May add more sauce if desired.)
- Spread vegetable mix on chicken breasts and sprinkle with 2-3 tablespoons of stuffing crumbs. Roll in jellyroll fashion and secure with toothpicks.
- Whip egg. Dip chicken in egg then roll in stuffing crumb mixture. Brown chicken in lightly oiled Dutch oven. Cover and cook 25-30 minutes until chicken is tender - internal chicken temperature should be 170°. Cook using 12 coals on top and 10-12 on the bottom - about 350°.
- Carefully remove toothpicks. Arrange on a bed of lacy greens on a Dutch oven lid. Drizzle with cheese sauce mixed with remaining milk to desired consistency. Sprinkle with paprika and garnish as desired.
- Serves 5.

STATE FAIR CHILI

- Melt: 1/2 cup butter
- Sauté until tender:
    2 yellow onions, chopped
    6 green onions, chopped
    1/2 of a green chili, seeded and chopped
    (May use entire chili if desired)
    2 cloves garlic, minced
- Remove vegetables and brown:
    3 pounds lean chili grind ground beef*
    1 pound pork sausage
- Drain off fat and stir in:
    1/2 cup flour
- Return vegetables to Dutch oven and add:
    1 4-ounce can pimentos
    3 pounds fresh tomatoes, chopped
    3/4 cup chopped celery
    1/2 pound fresh mushrooms, sliced
    1 sweet red pepper, chopped
    2 cups pitted ripe olives, chopped
    1/2 cup minced parsley
    1 12-ounce bottle Homestyle® chili sauce
- Simmer for 30 minutes then add:
    2 15 ounce cans pinto beans (optional)
    1 tablespoon garlic salt
    1 teaspoon black pepper
    2 teaspoons ground coriander
    1 tablespoon oregano
    2 tablespoons chili powder
- Simmer 1 – 11/2 hours.

You will need:

12" Deep Dutch Oven

30 Charcoal Briquets

Before serving add 1 cup sour cream (optional, but good).

Serves 10-12

This recipe won First Place at the Utah State Fair Chili Cook-off

For chili grind ground beef, call your local butcher and order in advance. If chili ground is not available, regular ground beef can be substituted.

Advanced

84

PERFECT PECAN CAKE

You will need:

10" Dutch Oven
(2 ovens or use one
twice for 2 layers)
20 Charcoal Briquets

Crust:

2 cups crushed vanilla wafers
1 cup chopped pecans
3/4 cup butter, softened

Cake:

2 1/2 cups flour or cake flour
1 cup granulated sugar
3/4 cup brown sugar, packed
1 teaspoon baking powder
1 teaspoon salt
1 teaspoon soda
4 eggs
3/4 teaspoon cinnamon
3/4 teaspoon allspice
1/2 teaspoon cloves
1/2 teaspoon nutmeg
1/2 cup buttermilk
1/4 cup butter
1 16 oz. can pumpkin

Topping:

1/2 cup whipping cream
1 cup pecan pieces
1 cup sugar
1/4 cube butter
1 egg
1 teaspoon vanilla

Serves 8-10

CRUST:

- In a large mixing bowl, combine wafer crumbs, and chopped pecans.
- Using a pastry cutter cut in butter until crumbly.
- Divide mixture in half and press one-half evenly on the bottom of a greased and floured 10-inch Dutch oven. Set the other half aside.

CAKE:

- In a large mixing bowl, mix cake ingredients until smooth.
- Divide mixture in half.
- Spread one-half on crumb mixture and bake approx. 350° (6 charcoal on the bottom and 14 on top) for 30-40 minutes until cake tests done. Cool 5 minutes; remove from pan and cool completely.
- Repeat procedure with other half of crumb mixture and cake mixture.

FILLING:

- 4-6 cups powdered sugar
- 2/3 cup softened butter
- 6 ounces cream cheese, softened
- 2 teaspoons vanilla
- Combine ingredients until light and fluffy. Spread between cake layers and frost cake.

TOPPING:

- Mix the cream, sugar and egg. Bring to a boil.
- Add pecan pieces and butter. Bring to a boil again. Remove from heat and add vanilla.
- Cool and drizzle over top of cake.
- Garnish with cherry and pecan halves.

APPLE CRUMB PIE

- Combine the first three ingredients and stir into apples.
- Line a buttered 10-inch Dutch oven with the pastry shell. Pour apple mixture into the shell.
- Combine remaining flour and sugar, then cut in the shortening until crumbly. Sprinkle over filling.
- Bake for 45-50 minutes with 14 coals on top and 6-8 on the bottom.

Basic Pie Crust - Single

- Lightly spoon flour into measuring cup and level without shaking or packing down. Combine flour and salt in a mixing bowl.
- With a pastry blender or two knives, cut in shortening until uniform; mixture should be coarse. Sprinkle with water, a tablespoon at a time; toss with a fork.
- Work dough into a firm ball with hands.
- Press dough into a flat circle with smooth edges.
- On a lightly floured surface, roll dough to a circle about 14-inches in diameter.
- Fold dough in half then fold in half again. Gently ease dough into oven, being careful not to stretch dough while unfolding it.
- Leave edges as they are until pie shell is filled. Trim edge about 1-inch above pie filling. Fold over and crimp edges or press with the tines of a fork.

You will need:

10" Dutch Oven

22 Charcoal Briquets

2/3 cup sugar

3/4 teaspoon cinnamon

2 tablespoons flour

6-8 Tart Apples, peeled, cored, grated

1 unbaked pastry shell (See below)

1/2 cup flour

1/4 cup brown sugar

1/4 cup butter

Basic Pie Crust - Single

1 1/3 cups sifted flour
1/2 teaspoon salt
1/2 cup butter-flavored Crisco®
3 tablespoons water

Serves 6-8

Advanced

ENCORE FUDGE CAKE

You will need:

Ultimate Dutch Oven®

OR

12" Deep Dutch oven with
   a Bundt pan

24 Charcoal Briquets

Serves 12-15

Glaze:

1 1/2 cups powdered sugar

Milk

• Mix powdered sugar with
   enough milk to make glaze
   of the desired consistency.

• Spoon glaze around the top of
   the cake and allow to drizzle
   down the sides.

• Garnish with chopped nuts
   and/or maraschino cherry
   halves, if desired.

• Sift together and set aside:
   2 1/4 cups all-purpose flour
   1/2 cup unsweetened cocoa
   1 1/2 teaspoons soda
   1 1/2 teaspoons baking powder
   1 teaspoon salt

• Beat together 1 minute:
   1 1/2 cups sugar
   3/4 cup oil
   2 eggs

• Mix wet and dry ingredients then add:
   3/4 cup water
   3/4 cup buttermilk
   1 teaspoon vanilla
   1/2 cup chopped nuts

• Filling:
   1 cup powdered sugar
   1 teaspoon vanilla
   4 ounces cream cheese
   1 egg
   2 tablespoons almond paste
   1/2 cup flaked coconut

• Spoon one-half of the batter into a greased and floured
   10-inch Bundt pan.

• Carefully spoon in filling to form a circle in the center
   of the batter. Do not let filling touch sides of pan.

• Top with remaining batter, place in Dutch oven and
   bake at 350° for 40-50 minutes or until cake tests done.

• Allow cake to cool for 10 minute. After 10 minutes
   invert on a Dutch oven lid. Allow the cake to cool for
   an additional 10 minutes then glaze.

GARNISHING

All garnishing should be edible.
Don't use plastic or paper unless it is typical, such as paper tassels on turkey legs. Doilies are okay under breads and desserts but we prefer using a nice black Dutch oven lid. If the bread or dessert has any moisture or is sticky, the paper will stick to the food.

Use edible flowers.
Those who like to use fresh flowers for garnishing should know which are edible. Some of the most popular choices are: borage, pansy, nasturtium, calendula, rosemary, fennel, squash blossoms and chives. Some grocery stores carry edible flowers. Do not use flowers from a florist, they have been treated with chemicals or pesticides which could contaminate the food. Flowers from a home garden should be raised organically with no pesticides and please make sure there are no resident insects. We attended one Cook-off where an entree was beautifully garnished with flowers from a home garden. On close inspection, aphids were crawling on the leaves (and in the food?). No thanks!

Garnishing should complement the dish.
For example: mint leaves add color to a rich chocolate brownie, but parsley springs would not be appropriate. Brownies could also be topped with a variety of sprinkles, drizzled with colored chocolate, an arrangement of nuts, or even some maraschino cherry halves for color. When possible, use ingredients that are incorporated in the dish.

Over-garnishing can be worse than no garnishing at all.
Check for color, size, texture and shape in garnishing. Garnishing should not be distracting so keep garnishes simple and eye appealing. When in doubt, leave it out.

On the next page are some simple suggestions.

Garnishing is the art of decorating a dish before presenting for serving. A well-garnished dish can have the psychological effect of making it taste better.

When preparing foods for family and friends, especially in the great outdoors, no one is expected to spend hours carving ice sculptures or forming intricate animal carvings from pumpkins. However, there are a few rules to remember that will help add that 'touch of class' to Dutch oven cooking.

Advanced

88

If using edible flowers in a contest, take documentation with you to the contest proving they are organically grown and are edible.

Green Onion Pom Poms

Select fresh green onions. Wash each onion and cut a 4-inch section up from the root end, then cut off the root. With a sharp knife, make 1 1/2-inch long cuts at 1/8-inch intervals around the bulb, cutting just to the center of the onion. Repeat on opposite end if desired. When both ends are complete, place in ice water until cut ends curl. It is best to use the bulb end of the onion for the contrast of white and green.

Tomato Rose

Select a medium to large firm red tomato. Use a sharp knife. Beginning at the non-stem end of the tomato, cut a paper-thin strip 3/4-inch wide. Continue cutting in one continuous spiral until the entire skin is removed. Begin at one end, winding the strip around itself, shaping the flower. Roll tightly at first relaxing as the rose gets bigger, folding the last piece underneath.

Cookie Cutters

Cookie cutters come in many sizes and shapes. They can be used to cut vegetables into leaves, flowers, etc. They can also be used to cut pie dough into beautiful shapes for topping pies or cutting a design in the top crust. Shapes can be cut in other baking ingredients such as phyllo dough. The imagination is the only limitation.

Unusual Vegetables

Spend some time in the produce section of the local supermarket. Notice lacy greenery in various colors. Experiment with different colors and textures of vegetables such as beets, daikon radishes, or jicama.

Onion Chrysanthemum

Select a white or yellow onion with a uniform shape. Remove the outside layer. Using a sharp knife, make cuts from the top to within 1/2-inch of the root end. Be careful not to cut through the root. Taper cuts to form petals, cutting to the center of the onion each time. Work around the onion until the entire onion has been cut.

Drop the onion root-side up in boiling water for approximately one minute to relax the petals. Then drop immediately into ice water, root-side down. Gently open petals. If color is desired, add food coloring until desired color is achieved. Keep in ice water until needed. Drain on a paper towel. Place in desired location.

COOKING FOR CROWDS

Good Dutch oven cooks are always at the top of the invitation list – "Oh, and could you bring your Dutch oven?" Plan on cooking for family reunions, church camp outs, even company parties where there will be large numbers of people. Don't be shy, share your talents.

Here are some tips when cooking for large groups:
Select simple recipes.

Don't choose recipes that require a lot of detailed steps unless there will be plenty of help and lots of time.

Make sure there is plenty of food. It is very embarrassing to run out of food before everyone is served. Plan for those who will want seconds. Add 10% above the actual number expected. The general rule of thumb is 1/2 pound of meat (raw, boneless, chicken, pork or beef) per person. This will average out between children, small eaters, large eaters and second helpings.

Don't cook too many dishes. Consider preparing the main dish, a potato side dish and a dessert. Buy rolls and salads or have people bring additional salads, relish trays, etc.

Get plenty of help. Only experienced cooks should try to prepare a meal by themselves. It is quite a juggling act to get everything cooked on time and have the serving table ready too.

Plan on surprises.

Expect things like weather problems, unavailable water or someone forgetting the key to the gate, etc. Allow extra time for such situations.

Plan as many details as possible on paper. Assign tasks well ahead so that inexperienced help will know what to expect. Will the tables need paper? Who's bringing the paper products? What needs to be done to keep the drinks cold? Will there be a covering if it rains? Is water available? Etc.

Those who enjoy cooking for crowds and would like to do some catering should check with the County Health Department for food-handler permits and regulations.

Advanced

ADAPTING RECIPES FOR CROWDS

As a rule, recipes requiring a

12-inch regular Dutch oven,

can be increased as follows:

$1\frac{1}{2}$ times = 12 Deep or 14
Regular

2 times = 14 Deep or 16
Regular

Keep notes from each cooking experience and make a list of items you will need. Here is ours:

Sanitizing solution (bleach & water) see food safety section
Salt & Pepper shakers
Mixing bowls with lids

Welding gloves	Matches, Gas lighter
Tablecloths	Aprons
Recipes	Dishpans
Dishcloths	Dishtowels
Dish soap	Band-Aids
Aspirin	Paper towels
Napkins	Paper plates
Cups	Salad plates
Dessert bowls	Knives
Forks	Spoons
Cooking oil	Cutting board
Other spices	Hot pads
Scissors	Tape
Toothpicks	Serving trays
Serving utensils	Tongs
Wire whisk	Ice cream scoop
Spatulas	Sharp knives
Measuring spoons	Measuring cups
Can opener	Baster
Lid stands	Meat thermometer
Handi wipes	Aluminum foil
Plastic bags	Prep table
Ice water	Charcoal
Lid lifter	Charcoal tongs
Whisk broom	Coal bucket and shovel

Be flexible. For all the reasons above, don't sweat the small stuff. If there is plenty of food and it is delicious, most folks will forgive a short delay.

Try to obtain larger ovens (14-inch and larger) for large groups. It is much easier to watch four large ovens than eight small ones.

ADDITIONAL INFORMATION

IDOS (International Dutch Oven Society)

Cooking Courtesy

Dutch Oven Cooking at Home

Cooking Outdoors

Organizing a Club

Hosting a Cook-off

Judging a Cooking Contest

As a Contestant

Fixing Problems

Safe Food Handling

Demonstrations

Emergency Preparedness

Thermometers

Conversions

Equivalents

IDOS is headquartered in Logan, Utah, and is a non-profit organization for promoting the art of Dutch oven cooking. Volunteers who are also Dutch oven cooks staff the organization.

IDOS

IDOS stands for International Dutch Oven Society.

It is headquartered in Logan, Utah, and is a non-profit organization for promoting the art of Dutch oven cooking. Volunteers who are also Dutch oven cooks staff the organization.

IDOS is in charge of the World Championship Dutch Oven Cook-off held in March at the Doug Miller Sportsmen's Exposition in Sandy, Utah. This Cook-off is an opportunity to see some of the best Dutch oven cooking in the world. There is also a spring convention usually held in March. Dutch oven cooks from all over gather to learn new techniques, see, taste and collect new recipes.

IDOS encourages DOGs (Dutch Oven Gatherings). Gather friends and neighbors, get out the Dutch oven's and have a social.

There are several Dutch oven societies including one in Japan (JDOS). If your area does not have a chapter, contact the IDOS and organize one. For valuable information and links to other sites, see www.idos.com.

World Wide Web

The Internet is a great information highway for all kinds of product and Dutch oven information. It is also a good source for recipes. Take advantage of it. Search under Dutch Oven, Cast Iron, Outdoor Cooking, Camp Chef, Etc.

Remember that once you have mastered the skills in this book, you can adapt almost any recipe for your Dutch oven. Don't limit yourself.

You can become a member of the International Dutch Oven Society.

Nationwide, groups meet to discuss cooking ideas, share recipes, compete in cooking contests and just to have fun!

To join, simply write in with your name and address and $15 membership fee (covers one full year) to:

IDOS, 41 E. 400 N. #210, Logan, UT 84321

Free Limited-Edition pin each year with membership

Additional Info.

DUTCH OVEN COOKING AT HOME

Cooking Courtesy

When cooking with others, use common courtesy. Always contain ashes so they do not blow into the neighbors cooking area or even worse, into their food.

Be helpful and willing to share food, recipes, ingredients, and ideas. That's the best way to learn and have fun with Dutch oven cooking.

With today's busy schedules, it's difficult to find time to create memories, but Dutch oven cooking is a great way to make a simple thing - like a meal - fun and memorable.

Some people believe Dutch oven cooking is a lot of work. If equipment and supplies are handy, you can prepare a meal in the same amount of time as cooking indoors. The difference is better flavor.

Almost anything that can be cooked in an indoor oven can be cooked in a Dutch oven outdoors. Have plenty of charcoal on hand. Keep supplies together in a specific location and ready to use so cooking can be done on a moment's notice.

Prepare the food indoors as usual then do the cooking on the patio or deck.

COOKING IN THE GREAT OUTDOORS

Dutch oven cooking is synonymous with outdoor cooking. Food preparation can be as simple or complicated as you like, but few people want to spend their playtime preparing food.

Once basic skills are mastered, perform the magic for family and friends. Share the talent at family reunions, camping trips, church socials, etc.

For a neighborhood or family cook out, have each family or guest bring a Dutch oven full of their favorite food. Or, if time allows, have everyone cook on site. This is a good time to get reacquainted with friends and relatives. It is a great way to learn new cooking tips and a good conversation starter.

By the time the food is ready, everyone is relaxed, comfortable and hungry.

Here are a few suggestions to make those outdoor meals easier:

Plan menus well in advance listing all ingredients needed.

Make sure all ingredients and preparation tools are handy.

Pre-measure, dice, chop, grate and package as much as possible beforehand so final mixing is quick. Have a copy of the recipe handy. (Don't trust your memory).

Using disposable containers reduces dishwashing time. Use Ziplock® bags to your advantage.

For proper food handling outdoors, see the section on food safety.

Pack ice chests tightly with at least one pound of ice for every pound of food. When possible, use two ice chests - one for drinks and one for food. The reason for this is to keep the food chest from being opened too often and releasing the cold.

If there are frozen foods, dry ice may be used.

ORGANIZING A CLUB

We started a Dutch oven club years ago and learned how to de-bone a chicken, secrets of sourdough breads, facts about and recipes using legumes, bread making tips and recipes, how to make tortillas, cuts of meats, etc. We even went on a few field trips. Learn things to do with cooking or whatever is interesting to the group. Have parties where everyone cooks and then evaluate the results. We shared our successes and our failures and made lifetime friendships in the process.

Friends who are interested in Dutch oven cooking and like to get together should consider organizing a club. Set up a yearly schedule, elect someone to be in charge, keep the group small and invite guest speakers. Decide how often to meet and stick with the schedule. Since everyone is busy, have a calling list to remind members of upcoming activities.

HOSTING A COOK-OFF

Folks who like friendly competition may want to get involved in hosting a Cook-off. These may range from a simple comparison of prepared foods to a big affair with judges and prizes. Here are some tips for a full-blown Cook-off. Use whatever information applies to your situation.

Decide how many dishes will be cooked. Should it be a 1, 2, or 3-pot Cook-off? Which categories will be cooked - main dishes, breads or desserts?

If the public is invited, provide a copy of the recipes. It is a good idea to collect the recipes in advance and put together a small cookbook, that can be sold to help offset costs. This cookbook will be helpful for judges during their evaluation of the cooking process and presentation of the final product.

Set a schedule and be punctual.

The following should be included: a set up time, judges meeting time, cooks meeting time, food-judging times and clean up time.

NOTE: For an IDOS sanctioned cook-off, contact IDOS for specific rules.

Sponsors

Running a contest costs money. Good sponsors will help pay for prizes and expenses.

When using sponsors, be sure to give them plenty of recognition and encourage contestants and bystanders to use their products. This is their only pay. Invite sponsors to participate in the Cook-off by judging or presenting prizes. Provide contestants with a list of the sponsor's names and addresses so they can write thank you notes. The sponsors will appreciate it.

Make it worthwhile to compete

It takes a lot of time and money to prepare to enter a Cook-off. The prizes should be worth the effort. If possible, give each team something just for coming to compete. Assign prizes for each category in advance to avoid trying to decide at the last minute what prizes go to what category and then later regret the decision. Contestants should know the prizes available in each category. Don't award prizes on a promise, make sure you have the prizes in your possession.

Start well in advance of the contest to organize a committee, arrange for sponsors and make sure every detail has been covered. Start a time line to allow plenty of time for planning, then follow it. Some locations require event permits as well as health department permits. Check with the local municipality to see what is required.

If experienced teams are competing, they probably have several Dutch ovens. Prizes relating to cooking supplies, equipment or cash may be a better choice than more Dutch ovens, unless they are specialty products.

Choose an appropriate location

A good place to host a Cook-off will have the following elements:

Be in conjunction with another event, which will help draw a crowd.

Have restroom facilities for contestants and public.

Have overhead coverings to protect from the hot sun or inclement weather.

Have a concrete or hard surface. In order to serve to the public, the Board of Health usually requires cooking to be done in an area that has a concrete or hard surface with an overhead covering. If possible, provide preparation tables and chairs for each of the teams.

Cordon off the cooking area to keep the public at a safe distance from the food preparation and hot charcoal.

Advertise. Advertise. Advertise.

There can never be too much advertising. Use the public service announcements available on TV and radio (depending on the size of the Cook-off, of course). Make posters and place in high traffic areas such as grocery stores or libraries.

Running a contest costs money. Good sponsors will help pay for prizes and expenses.

It takes a lot of time and money to prepare to enter a Cook-off. The prizes should be worth the effort.

There can never be too much advertising of your event.

Additional Info.

Supply badges or nametags for those involved in the competition for identification purposes. Limit the cooking area to those with ID tags to keep congestion to a minimum.

Get qualified judges

The majority of the judges should be experienced cooks with possibly two celebrities. Always have an odd number of judges (we suggest at least 5). Ask judges to remain after the contest to answer questions from contestants. There should be a judge's meeting for all judges before the contest. Judges should be notified and given all information well in advance. Assign one of the judges to be the Head Judge for final rulings and to answer any questions pertaining to judging protocol. This person should be an experienced Dutch oven cook.

Don't put judges on the spot. If there are judging problems, the head judge and the contest chairman should negotiate the resolution.

Train staff members to tally scores correctly. The judging sheets and scoring procedures suggested here will eliminate many problems.

Arrange for supplies and equipment

Make sure there are plenty of paper products appropriate for the dishes being judged; plates or bowls, plasticware, cups, and serving utensils. Have someone available to assist in serving the judges. Fruit, vegetables, and water should be provided for the judges to cleanse their palate when necessary during the tasting process.

If the Cook-off is an annual event, consider having a judging kit (a tool box works great for this) which will contain the following: sharp knives, instant read thermometer, serving knives, forks, and spoons, a small ladle, and pie servers.

Will the public get to sample? If so, make sure there are personnel and products (sampling cups) available to serve in a quick, orderly manner.

Arrange for safe food handling

It is the responsibility of the Cook-off committee to provide hot and cold running water for contestants. Make sure rules specify that all contestants must have both dishwashing facilities and hand washing facilities. (Hand sanitizers do not count.)

JUDGES QUALIFICATIONS

The best judges will have the following qualifications:

· Possess a wide knowledge of foods

· Have personal experience in many methods of food preparation

· Have personal ability to cook

· Possess the ability to recognize and reward excellence

· Have long term food memory so the first dish is equally evaluated with the last dish

· Have an appreciation of the efforts and expertise used to produce the results

· Have the ability to set aside food preferences and prejudices by judging every presentation on the merits, not on personal dislike for certain types of foods such as spinach

"Yes, I will judge a cooking contest. No, I have never done it before but how hard can it be? After all, I like to eat and have the figure to prove it."

Judging Procedures

Presentation of the food should include appropriate garnish, serving containers, color contrasts, harmony and edible decorations.

Reward pleasantly presented food.

Penalize gaudy garnishes that hide the food, or are not edible. Extra decor should not result in additional points or a higher placement. Ignore things that were not prepared with the recipe, such as an accompanying bottle of wine, freezer of ice cream or fine china.

Inspect the exterior of the food for color, symmetry of form, evenness of cooking, volume, and surface texture such as the golden brown rolls with a crisp crust and evenly browned meat. Penalize spotty cooking, burned spots, raw, tough, soggy, brittle, or crumbling results.

Internal inspection. Dig in and look at the bottom.

Use a thermometer to insure that cooking temperatures meet food safety guidelines. Hot foods should be above 140°. Cold foods should be below 40°. Oh, what a wonderful variety of things grow in the food at temperatures between 40° and 140°!

Seek to discover areas that are raw, under-cooked, burned, off color, or tough. Reward pleasant aroma, uniform color, evenness of cooking, consistent texture, and completeness of the cooking process. Penalize problems such as burned spots, raw spots, streaks, or lumps.

Taste

"The proof of the pudding is in the eating!" This is the most important factor in judging. The contest is for the best cooking, not the best decorating. As a judge, you owe the contestants a clear palate that has no lingering flavors from previous foods. A drink of water, a grape, or a dry cracker may help remove lingering flavors such as pepper or chocolate.

As a judge, you should have a strong desire to taste this presentation, especially if you have just tasted many items that are similar. The ideal is that the food tastes delicious. Reward pleasant use of spices, natural food flavors, evenness of cooking, chewability and aroma. A tip on aroma: When the food is in the mouth, breathe in through the mouth and out through the nose. The many aroma sensors in the nose will tell you a lot about the food. Penalize for toughness, off flavors, rancid oil flavor, burned food, foreign objects, ash, flatness, unwanted lumps, spotty cooking, cold spots, raw spots, missing ingredients, unnatural food colors, and soggy crusts.

Use a thermometer to insure that cooking temperatures meet food safety guidelines. Hot foods should be above 140°. Cold foods should be below 40°. Oh, what a wonderful variety of things grow in the food at temperatures between 40° and 140°!

Use serving utensils only when collecting taste samples. Do not cross-contaminate foods by putting your tasting utensil into the foods being judged.

GENERAL CHARACTERISTICS OF GREAT FOOD

Breads

The mastering of cooking techniques is well demonstrated in the baking of breads. The size of the loaves or rolls should be uniform, the rise should be even, and the baking color should be a uniform golden brown on the top, sides and the bottom. The crumb should have some luster. The aroma should have a fresh quality. The texture should be even and not coarse. Sourdough breads may have a coarse texture due to rapid production of gas, but should be even in texture. Fine quality ingredients help achieve superior results. Innovative recipes combine a various array of ingredients to produce an exciting taste result.

Desserts

A great dessert is more than sweet. Fresh ingredients assist the dessert in having distinctive flavors and a variety in consistency. Sauces used in desserts should carry a flavor experience in a tight clear manner. Runny sauces with lumps and an off flavor are not desirable. Piecrusts should be evenly brown, crisp and flaky. Cakes should have a fine texture, even doneness, and an exciting flavor. Fruits should have a fresh flavor and an easy eating consistency.

Meat Main Dishes

Meat should be selected for tenderness, fine flavor and uniform cut. The cooking should present the meat hot, tender and moist. Beef goes tough as it cools. Spices and flavors may be added by marinades and during cooking. Beef is often cooked directly on the bottom of the oven in a moist heat. Pork and lamb are best cooked on a rack to enable the fat to drain away from the meat during cooking. Chicken should be tender and moist when served. Choose cuts of meat that have lesser amounts of fat. Fish should be flaky and moist.

Vegetable Main Dishes

Jump right into the debate between soft and soggy versus crisp and tough cooked vegetables. The final condition should result in the flavorful, colorful vegetables being easy to eat. Strong vegetable flavors such as onions or cauliflower should be muted in the preparation and cooking process. Exciting combinations of vegetables and other ingredients are resulting in many tempting main dishes.

Breads

The mastering of cooking techniques is well demonstrated in the baking of breads. The size of the loaves or rolls should be uniform, the rise should be even, and the baking color should be a uniform golden brown on the top, sides and the bottom.

Desserts

A great dessert is more than sweet. Fresh ingredients assist the dessert in having distinctive flavors and a variety in consistency.

Meat Main Dishes

Meat should be selected for tenderness, fine flavor and uniform cut. The cooking should present the meat hot, tender and moist.

Vegetable Main Dishes

The final condition should result in the flavorful, colorful vegetables being easy to eat. Strong vegetable flavors such as onions or cauliflower should be muted in the preparation and cooking process.

Additional Info.

Beware of the Big Helping

Small servings give the taste that you require to adequately judge the flavor. Be hungry for the last sample. The alternative is to be stuffed part way through the tasting. Forcing food down will unfairly influence your judging.

Judging Standards

Look for dishes that are the best you have ever eaten. Ask yourself, "Would I be proud to serve this to any of my guests?" A winner should be a good example of all-around quality not just a gimmick.

From the Article, "Judging Dutch Oven Cooking". Prepared by A. Glen Humpherys, Ph.D. Former Curator - Director of Wheeler Historic Farm, Dutch oven instructor, contestant, judge, and enthusiast. Special contributions were made by Gerry Duffin and Chauna Duffin. They are both experienced Dutch Oven cooks and successful contestants.

FOOD JUDGING SCORE SHEET (Sample)

BREADS

TEAM#_____
NAME OF DISH_____

Circle One: 1st (5 points)
                  2nd (4 points)
                  3rd (3 points)
                  4th (2 points)
                  5th (1 point)

Judges will write in the team number and the name of the dish prepared. No matter how many teams are entered, only the top five will be considered for final evaluation. This process of elimination is relatively simple:

· The judges look at ALL the dishes first, noting those that are overly garnished, misshapen, or beautifully done following the judging guidelines above. They will be watching to see if they are presented according to the rules and with creativity.

· Next they will check aromas. Are there any off odors, anything too strong, etc.

· Finally they will dig in, giving each dish a chance to impress them. As they go through this process the best dishes will stand out.

- When they have eliminated all but five, they may evaluate those five dishes again to decide which placement on the score sheet they feel applies.

After the judging sheets are filled out, it is a simple matter to tally the scores and announce the winners. For accuracy there should be at least two people tallying score sheets.

FIELD JUDGING

The purpose of field judging is:

- To see that all contestants follow rules of cleanliness and proper food handling.
- To evaluate techniques used during food preparation and cooking.
- To observe sportsmanship and public interaction of participating teams.
- To assist contestants by offering suggestions, if asked.

Field Judge Scoring

Each team will begin with three points. A field judge may subtract points for flagrant violations of cleanliness rules, poor cooking techniques or bad sportsmanship. The judge may add points for exceptional technique or great sportsmanship and public interaction.

The score may not exceed five points or go below zero points. An item receiving a zero is disqualified and may not be presented for judging.

Caution: Be aware that the teams have gone to a lot of work to participate. The encouragement and positive suggestions of a field judge may be the key to an enjoyable and successful cooking experience.

Please reserve a zero score for items, which are truly not edible and could cause illness if tasted.

FIELD JUDGING RESPONSIBILITIES

- Read the recipes. Are contestants following the recipe? No secret ingredients should be used. (Garnishing items do not have to be included in the recipe.)
- Check for clean food preparation practices.
  See that all food cooked is presented to the judges.
- Check for good sportsmanship and public interaction.

If unsafe foods are discovered during judging, they should be discretely removed from the judging table and returned to the team. Unsafe foods should never be sampled or served to the public. (See Food Safety Section.)

- Read the recipes.
- Check for clean food preparation.
- Check for good sportsmanship.
- Test meat temperatures before serving.
- Only recipe ingredients should be cooked during the competition.

Before disqualifying any team, meet with the other field judges and discuss the violations to make sure all judges agree!

Additional Info.

WATCH FOR:

- Cleanliness

- All cooked items must be

  presented

- Demonstrate good

  sportsmanship

- Use the best cooking

  techniques available

- Meats should be cooked to

  the correct temperatures

ONLY USDA INSPECTED

MEATS SHOULD BE

SERVED TO THE PUBLIC.

- Only contestants should be

  allowed in the cooking area.

· Test meat temperatures before serving.

· Only recipe ingredients should be cooked during the competition. (No private meals.)

· It is acceptable for field judges to offer suggestions and encouragement if requested by the teams.

· Give a warning before deducting points unless there is a flagrant violation of clean cooking practices. Some teams are concentrating so much on their task, they may not be aware of a rule violation or food preparation problem.

NOTE: Cook-off winners should be chosen for their skills in Dutch oven cooking. The Food should be the focus.

The purpose of field judging is to insure the food is safe for judges and the public, not to determine the winners.

CONTEST RULES

Cleanliness is the key. Start with clean equipment and use clean cooking practices. Wash hands often.

All items cooked must be presented to the judges. If a field judge notices flagrant rule violations, that team could be disqualified. Nothing burned or undercooked should be removed and discarded prior to judging. Note: If the item is undercooked or cannot be presented on time, contestants should withdraw their entry.

Demonstrate good sportsmanship. Interaction with the public is an important part of the cooking contest. Be courteous and willing to answer questions. Please promote sponsors and their products - they have made the competition possible.

Use the best cooking techniques possible.

Meats should be cooked to the following temperatures:

    a. Beef - 145° for at least 15 seconds

    b. Pork, ground beef, game meat - 155° for at least 15 seconds

    c. Poultry, fish and foods stuffed with meat - 165° for at least 15 seconds

These temperatures are from the FDA as of October 15, 1996.

ONLY USDA INSPECTED MEATS SHOULD BE SERVED TO THE PUBLIC. Avoid any home-processed items.

To avoid confusion, only CONTESTANTS should be allowed in the cooking area.

Please do not:......

......lick fingers when preparing food (unless hands are washed immediately).

......taste foods and then use the same utensil to stir food without washing it.

......place cooking utensils on unclean surfaces.

......cross-contaminate foods by placing uncooked meats on a cutting board then placing raw vegetables on the same cutting board without washing it in between.

......place Dutch oven lids on the ground.

......use the same tongs for handling food and charcoal.

AS A CONTESTANT

Enjoy fellow contestants and the public. Have fun!

Skillful garnishing can cover some surface imperfections.

The first contest will be a great learning experience. If not as successful as hoped, don't get discouraged, experience leads to success.

Those who decide to enter a contest will want to consider the following:

Choose great recipes. Select recipes that taste fantastic, show well and can be garnished on site. (There are some garnishing and presentation tips in the cooking section of this book.) The judging section describes judging protocol.

Don't buy generic ingredients unless sure of the quality.

It is better to cook something simple to perfection than to cook something difficult and have problems.

Make sure all equipment is clean and in good condition, especially the Dutch ovens. The public is coming to see a show.

Use proper food handling procedures. Nobody wants to make the judges sick! (See Safe Food Handling section)

Know the rules. Ignorance is no excuse. Read and understand all rules before cooking. Any questions should be asked during the Contestants Meeting prior to the start of the contest.

Cook the recipe several times at home to check for timing, ingredients, garnishing and taste. Timing is very important. Choose recipes that can be done in the time allowed.

Plan for the unexpected. Cooking conditions may include windstorms, rain, snow or intense heat. Under those conditions, how will the recipes fare? What adaptations will be needed in case these problems occur?

When the contest is over, ask judges for positive suggestions. Remember, winning a contest means that on a particular day, a certain dish pleased the palate of that panel of judges. This changes from judge to judge, contest to contest and day to day. Contests do not really prove one contestant superior to another. It is better to enter for the fun of cooking, winning is a bonus.

FIXING PROBLEMS

It is impossible to foresee every difficulty encountered when cooking Dutch oven, and some things just can't be fixed, but here are some suggestions to remedy the most common problems.

If rolls or yeast breads are not rising, place about 4 coals on the lid. This should provide enough heat for the yeast to work. In very hot weather, be sure to keep ovens out of direct sunlight. Temperatures in a black pot on a hot day can be high enough to kill the yeast.

If a cake has fallen, redistribute the charcoal placing heat in the center of the top to bring it back up. Check food often after the first 20 minutes (but not before). Waiting too long to act on a problem may make it impossible to remedy the situation.

Use your senses. An experienced cook can tell how the food is cooking by watching, listening and smelling the food during the cooking process. Stir stews and soups often to keep them from scorching on the bottom. If items are only slightly scorched, do not scrape the bottom of the pot. Serve only edible foods. Remember, in a Cook-off removing burned food is against the rules. (This is one reason practice is so important.)

If the food is not browning evenly, rearrange the heat. Checking often is a habit of good cooks.

When it's all said and done, if you've ruined a dish, our friend Ruth Kendrick says, "Just re-name it!"

Additional Info.

SAFE FOOD HANDLING

We have recently learned that hand sanitizers are no substitute for hand washing. Do not rely on them as the only source for clean hands.

Remember food safety--foods maintaining temperatures between 40 degrees F. and 140 degrees F. for longer than two hours are not safe to serve.

Now, more than ever, it is important to use good food handling practices. Food poisoning, parasites and diseases can be spread through improper food handling.

Keep it Clean

Wash Hands:
- In hot soapy water for 20 seconds
- Dry with a paper towel

Always wash hands after:
- Using the bathroom
- Changing diapers
- Petting animals
- Coughing or sneezing into hand
- Blowing nose
- Smoking

And always before handling food

Sanitize Frequently
- Counter tops and equipment
- Cutting boards (use plastic, not wood)
- Scrubbers/brushes
- Sanitizing solution–1 tablespoon chlorine bleach in 1 gallon warm water (75° F.)

It is a good idea to keep this solution in a spray bottle for convenient use.

How to Wash Dishes and Utensils
- Scrape
- Pre-rinse
- Wash and scrub in hot (120°) soapy water
- Rinse in hot water
- Sanitize (75°) solution (see above)
- Air dry

Cook food to the proper temperature

· Always use an instant read thermometer to ensure safe food serving temperatures.
· Hot foods should be kept above 140°
· Cold foods should be kept below 40°
· Cool large quantities in smaller containers
· Avoid raw eggs - keep them refrigerated
· Thaw meats in the refrigerator or cold water bath
· Stuff poultry just before cooking or bake stuffing separately
· Put leftovers in the refrigerator immediately

Any food left above 40° or below 140° longer than two hours is not considered safe to eat.

When in doubt, throw it out!

We recommend a County Board of Health food handlers class for everyone who cooks. It usually only takes a few hours and is well worth the effort.

Call your County Board of Health for information.

Caution: Heating does not destroy Staph toxins. Do not rely on reheating leftovers to make mishandled food safe. Freezing does not kill bacteria in food; it simply stops their growth.

Additional Info.

RECOMMENDED INTERNAL TEMPERATURES

Product	Degrees Fahrenheit
Eggs & Egg Dishes	
Eggs	Yolk & white are firm
Egg dishes	160°
Ground Meat and Poultry Mixtures	
Turkey, Chicken (including patties)	165°
Veal, beef, lamb, pork (including patties)	160°
Fresh Beef	
Medium rare	145°
Medium	160°
Well done	170°
Fresh Lamb	
Medium rare	145°
Medium	160°
Well done	170°
Fresh Pork	
Medium	160°
Well done	170°
Poultry	
Chicken, whole	180°
Turkey, whole	180°
Poultry breasts, roasts	170°
Poultry thighs, wings	180°
Stuffing	165°
Duck and goose	180°
Ham	
Fresh (raw)	160°
Pre-cooked (to reheat)	140°

These temperatures are recommended for consumer cooking. They are not intended for processing, institutional, or food service preparation.

DEMONSTRATIONS

Good Dutch oven cooks are often asked to do a demonstration for local businesses to sell their products. If asked to do a demonstration, here are some tips:

Keep yourself, hands and equipment and cooking area clean.

Make sure there is plenty of food and serving utensils.

If it is advertised from 10:00 a.m. to 2:00 p.m., go early and be cooking by ten and be sure to have something to serve until two.

Understand and be familiar with the products being demonstrated.

Keep foods simple so time can be spent talking to people. They will have many questions – be available to answer them.

Do as much as possible to prepare in advance.

Take lots of water to drink. There is often not enough time to eat when demonstrating but it is important to drink plenty of water.

The company sponsoring the demonstration should provide any permits and proper facilities to meet board of health regulations.

Contact Camp Chef for a free demo guide.
1-800-650-2433.

EMERGENCY PREPAREDNESS

"Be Prepared!" It's good advice for everyone, not just the Boy Scouts. When the recent Y2K concern was in full swing, items that were portable and needed no electricity were in big demand. Dutch ovens and related equipment were among those items.

For minor inconveniences like a power outage, a Dutch oven, some charcoal and a safe place to cook will provide a good meal while neighbors are eating peanut butter sandwiches.

During a major emergency, several families could share their resources with one family providing the main dish, one a bread or side dish and another the dessert. This would provide more than nutrition in a difficult situation; it would foster cooperation and support.

An emergency is not the time to pull a new Dutch oven out of the box and find out it needs to be seasoned while a hungry family looks on. Take time now to learn the basics and acquire needed equipment and skills.

THERMOMETERS

When buying a thermometer, the 0° to 220° model will meet most cooking needs. (Deep-frying needs 0° to 550°.)

Deciding whether a particular food is done is sometimes a matter of opinion. So, for matters of safety, it is important to use a thermometer to be sure foods are cooked to an internal temperature high enough to destroy any bacteria that may have been in the food. Contrary to popular opinion, color is not a reliable way to determine if a food is properly cooked.

Rather than list all of the different types of thermometers, we are recommending the type we use, the 'Instant Read'. The Instant Read thermometer has the following characteristics:

It can register the internal temperature of food in 15 to 20 seconds.

It has a wide range of uses.

It can be used to check the internal temperatures of foods at any time during the cooking process.

The temperature is averaged along 2 to 3-inches of the probe. In order to get a correct reading; the probe needs to be inserted at least 2 to $2^{1/2}$-inches into the food. For proper testing, layer thin cuts of meat 2 to $2^{1/2}$-inches thick, or insert the probe in sideways to the correct depth.

Instant read thermometers do just that - give an instant reading. They are not manufactured to be left in the meat or in the oven for extended periods.

Buy a good quality model with the calibration nut on the back. To calibrate an instant read thermometer, fill a large glass with finely crushed ice. Add clean tap water to the top of the ice and stir. Place the stem of the thermometer at least 2-inches into the mixture without touching the sides or bottom of the glass. After a minimum of 30 seconds and while still in the ice mixture, hold the adjusting nut under the head of the thermometer with a suitable tool and turn the head until the pointer reads 32°F.

Look for an easy-to-read dial.

CONVERSIONS

Recipe Calls For	*You May Use*
1 qt. covered saucepan	8" Dutch oven
2 qt. covered saucepan	8" Dutch oven
3 qt. covered saucepan	10" Dutch oven
4 qt. covered kettle	10" Dutch oven
6 qt. covered kettle	12" Dutch oven
9" pie plate	10" Dutch oven
12 x 7^{1}/2 x 2 baking dish	10" Dutch oven
13 x 9 x 2 baking dish	12" Dutch oven
8 x 8 x 2 baking dish	8" Dutch oven
9 x 9 x 2 baking dish	10" Dutch oven
10" tube pan	10" Dutch oven, foil covered tube in centre , or 12" UDO®
Bundt Pan	12" Deep, foil covered tube in center, or 14" UDO®

When converting a recipe from a regular cookbook to Dutch oven, use this chart as a general guide. Remember that adjustments must be made for depth changes in some cases. Example: a pie, which fits in a 9-inch pie plate, can be placed in a 10-inch Dutch oven.

If ingredients are thicker than the original recipe, add 25% more cooking time. If shallower, deduct 25%.

Additional Info.

114

EQUIVALENTS

Measurements

Pinch = 1/8 teaspoon or less

Dash = 1/8 teaspoon or less

1 tablespoon = 3 teaspoons

1/4 cup = 4 tablespoons.

1/3 cup = 51/2 tablespoons

1 cup = 16 tablespoons

1 cup = 8 fluid ounces

1 fluid ounces = 2 tablespoons

Half pint. = 1 cup

1 pint = 2 cups

1 quart = 4 cups or 2 pints.

1 gallon = 4 quarts

Peck = 8 quarts

Bushel = 4 pecks

Amounts

1 stick butter = 1/2 cup

1 cup cream = 2 cups whipped cream

1 pound cheese = 4-5 cups grated cheese

1 large onion = approximately 1 cup chopped

1 large green pepper = approximately 1 cup diced

1 orange = 1/3 to 1/2 cup juice

1 orange rind, grated = approximately 1 tablespoon

1 lemon = approximately 2 tablespoons juice

1 lemon rind, grated = approximately 1 teaspoon

1 medium apple = 1 cup sliced

1 medium banana = 1/3 cup mashed

1 medium peach = 1/2 cup sliced

4 cups whole strawberries = 4 cups sliced

1 medium tomato = 1/2 cup chopped

1 pound uncooked rice = 2 cups cooked

1 cup uncooked rice = approximately 3 cups cooked

1 pound nuts = approximately 2 cups nutmeats

1 pound sugar = 2 cups

1 pound powdered sugar = 3 1/2 to 4 cups

1 pound packed brown sugar = 2 1/4 cups

1 pound sifted all-purpose flour = 4 cups

1 pound butter or margarine = 2 cups

1 cup finely crushed graham crackers = 14 squares

All-purpose flour, 1 pound = 4 cups

1 slice bread = 1/4 cup dry crumbs

1 cup fine cracker crumbs = 28 saltine crackers

1 cup fine wafer crumbs = 22 vanilla wafers

1 tablespoon fresh herbs = 1/3 to 1/2 tsp. dried

1 cup honey = 1 1/4 cups sugar plus 1/4 cup liquid

1 pound potatoes = 3 medium sized potatoes

1 package active dry yeast = 1 tablespoon yeast

#303 can = 2 cups or 16-17 ounces

#2 can = 2 1/2 cups or 20 ounces

#10 can = 12 to 13 cups (same as 7 #303 cans)

USE THIS PAGE TO MAKE NOTES

APPENDIX

Glossary
Recipe Index
Index

Appendix

Fried Chicken, page 51

THANK YOU FOR PURCHASING THIS BOOK

If you have learned something new, been inspired to try new recipes or purchased and seasoned an oven, our work has not been in vain.

If you have successes, failures or funny stories about Dutch oven cooking you'd like to share, or if you have wonderful recipes or comments and suggestions about this book, we'd love to hear from you. Please contact us at:

Gerry and Chauna Duffin
C/O Camp Chef
P. O. Box 4057
Logan, UT   84323-4057

For additional recipes, see "The Friends of Old Deseret Dutch Oven Cookbook". This book is a compilation of nine years of Cook-off recipes from This is the Place State Park in Salt Lake City, Utah.

GLOSSARY

Acidic Foods - Foods, such as tomatoes, which are high in acid content. These foods react with aluminum cookware causing undesirable colors and flavors. These foods can also break down the patina of cast iron cookware if improperly seasoned.

Bail - The wire handles on the pot of a Dutch oven.

Capacity - The amount a Dutch oven can hold, usually measured to the rim.

Casting - The process of pouring molten metal into a form to create a Dutch oven

Cured - Seasoned

D.O.G. - Dutch Oven Gathering.

Emery cloth - A fabric backed sandpaper used for sanding and polishing metal.

Flanged lid - The raised lip on a camp oven that prevents ashes and charcoal from falling off the lid.

Headroom/headspace - The area in a Dutch oven between the food and the lid.

Patina - The slick non-stick surface of cast iron created by filling the pores of the metal with a coating of oil and/or seasoning product then baking at a high temperature.

Rancid - The odor of oils used in cooking or seasoning which have become stale.

Seasoned/Seasoning - See patina.

Self-basting - A Dutch oven lid which has several small protrusions on the underside. As moisture evaporates, it is collected and drips back onto the food.

Surfactant - Surface cleaner.

Valve-lapping Compound - An automotive paste-like abrasive compound used to polish rough surfaces of metals.

Ventilation - Air flow.

Warp - Overheating metal to the point where it loses its original shape.

RECIPE INDEX

All-American Baked Beans 54

Almost Pumpkin Pie 73

Apple Crumb Pie 86

Applesauce Bread 65

APPLES
    Apple Crumb Pie 86
    Applesauce Bread 65

Barbecued Chicken or Ribs 53

Basic Cornbread 48

BEANS
    All-American Baked Beans 54
    State Fair Chili 84

Best Ever Cinnamon Rolls 81

Biscuit-topped Chili 46, 68

BREADS
    Applesauce Bread 65
    Basic Cornbread 48
    Best Ever Cinnamon Rolls 81
    Dinner Rolls 64
    Flaky Baking Powder Biscuits 46
    Frozen Rolls 49
    Marie's Fabulous French Rolls 66

BREAKFAST
    Breakfast Casserole 50
    Egg Soufflé 67

CAKES
    Encore Fudge Cake 87
    Perfect Pecan Cake 85

CHICKEN
    Barbecued Chicken or Ribs 53
    Fried Chicken 51
    Golden Cashew Chicken 83
    Sweet Chicken Delight 53

DESSERTS
    Almost Pumpkin Pie 73
    Apple Crumb Pie 86
    Best Ever Cinnamon Rolls 81
    Coconut Brownie 70

Cobblers 57
Crown Cobbler 71
Encore Fudge Cake 87
Favorite Fruit Roll 72
Perfect Pecan Cake 85

Dinner Rolls 64
Dutch Oven Potatoes 55
Egg Soufflé 67
Encore Fudge Cake 87
Favorite Fruit Roll 72
Flaky Baking Powder Biscuits 46
Fried Chicken 51
Frozen Rolls 49
Gerry's Stir Fry 52
Golden Cashew Chicken 83
Grandma's Great Potatoes 69
Honey Butter 48

MAIN DISHES
All-American Baked Beans 54
Barbecued Chicken or Ribs 53
Biscuit-topped Chili 46, 68
Dutch Oven Potatoes 55
Fried Chicken 51
Gerry's Stir Fry 52
Golden Cashew Chicken 83
Grandma's Great Potatoes 69
More Than Taco Soup 69
Savory Stuffed Pork Roast 82
State Fair Chili 84
Sweet Chicken Delight 53

Marie's Fabulous French Rolls 66
More than Taco Soup 69
Perfect Pecan Cake 85

PIES
Apple Crumb Pie 86

PORK
Savory Stuffed Pork Roast 82

PUMPKIN
Almost Pumpkin Pie 73
Perfect Pecan Cake 85

Rhodes 49, 57, 71
Ribs 53
Savory Stuffed Pork Roast 82

State Fair Chili 84

Stir Fry, Gerry's 52

Sweet Chicken Delight 53

GENERAL INDEX

Acidic foods 11, 121

Altitude, high 30

Aluminum Dutch Oven 10, 11, 13, 15, 21, 23, 40, 41, 121

Aluminum Foil 16, 44, 45, 78, 91

Alzheimer's and aluminum 11

Baking 10, 17, 30, 33, 36, 45

Barbecue, seasoning method 20

Boiling 25, 34, 35, 40

Box, for transporting 29

Burned food 25, 101, 108

Burying an oven 36

Camp Chef
   Cleaner 19, 21, 22, 27, 40
   Conditioner 19-23,27, 40
   Method of seasoning (See Seasoning Section page 18)
   Dutch ovens 12, 15
   Dutch oven chart 14, 15
   Products 19, 20, 21, 22, 27, 28, 40, 41, 51, 52, 112

Camp oven, chart 14, 15

Camp oven, definition of 11

Campfire cooking 21, 24, 25, 36, 38

Camping 10, 32, 38, 47, 51, 95

Cast iron, benefits of 10, 11, 12

Cast iron, characteristics of 10, 11, 12, 18, 25,

Casting 10, 17, 121

Charcoal
  Disposing of 29, 35
  Storing 34

Charcoal basket 28, 35

Charts

   Camp Chef products 15

   Camp ovens 14, 15

   Conversions 114
   Dutch ovens 14, 15

   Equivalents 114

   Food temperatures 111
   MACA ovens 14

Chimney starter 28

Choosing an oven 12

Cleaning Dutch ovens 22-23

Appendix

124

Club, organizing a 97

Cold weather, cooking in 31

Competition 77, 107

Conditioner, Camp Chef 19-23, 27-40

Conversion chart 114

Conventional oven, seasoning in 21

Cookbooks 7, 27, 63, 76, 120

Cooking tables 27, 30

Covers, Dutch oven 28

Cracked ovens 23-25

Crowds, cooking for 6, 90, 91, 98

Do's and Don'ts 22-23

Dutch oven,
    Chart s 14, 15
       Dutch oven, definition of 11
       Dutch oven, history 10
       Dutch oven materials 11

Emergency preparedness 112

Equivalents 115-116

Family reunions 90, 95

Field judging 104, 106

Fire Safety 38

First aid 38

Food handling, safe 26, 96, 99, 104, 107, 109

Frequently asked questions 16-17, 24-25

Frying 34, 35, 40, 113

Garnishing 44, 88-89, 106-107

Glossary 121

Gloves 18, 26, 77, 91

Good food, characteristics of 102

Griddle, using lid as 9, 13

Grub box 29

Heat-resistant surface 27

Heat Sources
    Buffalo Chips 37
    Charcoal 16, 17, 30-36, 38, 40, 41
    Conventional oven 16, 17, 20, 21, 37
    Firewood 17,21, 35-36
    Propane 13, 17, 20, 24, 28, 35, 41

History, Dutch oven 10

Home, cooking at 37, 95

Hot weather, cooking in 31

Humidity, cooking in 31

ID tags 29

Indoor uses 16

Judging good food 6, 100-105

Judging, competition 6, 99-105

Kitchen cooking 37

Lard, for seasoning 20

Lid, fitting 17, 25

Lid lifter 26
Lid-stand 26

Lighter fluid 28, 34

Lodge Manufacturing 12, 14

MACA Supply 14

Metallic taste 19, 24

Neighborhood cookouts 95

Oil, for seasoning 20, 23

Outdoor Cooking 11, 95

Oven capacities 14, 15

Patina, definition of 18

Paul Revere 10

Propane stoves 20, 34, 35

Purchasing 17

Questions, frequently asked 16-17, 24-25
Rain, cooking in 31

Rancid ovens 19, 22, 23, 25, 121

Roasting 34

Rough casting 17

Rusty ovens 24

Sanitizing solution, homemade 109

Scoring, Cook-off 103-104

Seasoning cast iron 18-21
    Barbecue method 20
    Camp Chef method 19
    Flaking 24
    Products 19, 20, 40
    Methods 19-21

Self-cleaning oven 19, 24

Shortening, seasoning with 20

Simmering 34

Snow, cooking in 31

Specialty ovens 13

Specialty oven chart 14-15

Starter fluid 28, 34

Steaming 34, 40

Sticky ovens 18, 23, 25

Storing ovens 19, 23, 28

Sunshine, cooking in 31

Temperatures, for doneness 101, 105, 110, 111

Thermometer 29, 113
    Use of 101, 109, 113

Tongs 26

Appendix

126

Tools 26-29

Ultimate Dutch Oven 12, 13, 15, 40, 41

Variables 30-31
    Altitude 30, 47, 62, 63
    Wind 30
    Cold 31
    Heat 31
    Humidity 31
    Snow 31
    Rain 31
    Sunshine 31

Whisk broom 28, 29, 91

Wind, cooking in 30

Wire rack 28